Little Women

**Common Core Aligned Unit for Grades 5-12
Includes Non-Fiction Readings and Lessons**

With Differentiated Vocabulary

By Elizabeth Chapin-Pinotti © 2013

ISBN: 978-0615862637

(c) 2013 Lucky Willy Publishing. All rights reserved. No part of this publication may be reproduced or transmitted in any form or by any means without written permission from the publisher; however, the photos herein that are in the Public Domain may be copied and distributed. Copies for classroom use may also be made. Requests for permission to copy please email: publisher@luckyjenny.com

Table of Contents

Introduction	page 5
Character List	page 6

Chapter by Chapter Think and Writes

Chapter 1: Compare and Contrast	page 8
Chapter 1: Active Reading Making Inferences	pages 9-10
Chapter 2: Historical Context: Non-Fiction	pages 11-14
Chapter 3: Critical Thinking	page 15
Chapter 4: Character Burdens	page 16
Chapter 5: Character Traits and Motives	page 17
Chapter 6: Critical Thinking	page 18
Chapter 7: Civil War Critical Thinking	page 19
Chapter 8: The Ideal of Womanhood – Women in the 1860s	page 20
Chapter 9: Social Studies Tie-In Reading and Writing	page 21-23
Chapter 10: The P.C. and the P.O. and Your Life	page 24
Chapter 11: Real World Tie-In Transcendentalists	page 25
Chapter 12: Camp Laurence – Your Life	page 26
Chapter 13: Foreshadowing	page 27
Chapter 13: Literature and Your Life	page 28
Chapter 14: Your Future Dreams – Your Castles	page 29
Chapter 15: Questions with Personal Tie-In	page 30
Chapter 16: Your Letter to Marmee	page 31
Chapter 17: Penicillin: Science Tie-In	page 32
Chapter 17: Science Experiment – Growing Mold	page 33
Chapter 18: My Dark Event	page 34
Chapter 19: Conflict and Graphic Novel Activity	page 35
Chapter 20: Confidential: My Bundle of Naughties	page 36
Chapter 21: Critical Thinking	page 37
Chapter 22: What Would My Gift's Be	page 38
Chapter 23: My Predictions for the Future	page 39

My Little Notebook Instructions	page 40-56

1. **Literary Terms**: Throughout the reading.
2. **What is Your Favorite Literary Term and Why** – Halfway through the reading
3. **Write and Think: You and the Novel. Which Character Are You Most Like?** – After Chapter 10
4. **What I Think: Are the Character's Likeable?** – Anytime after Chapter 3 (you may want to include this page twice and have students re-do it at the end of the story and compare to see if their perspective changed).
5. **Social Studies Tie-In: Feminist Literature Non-Fiction Read and Write** – Anytime after Chapter 14 (2-3 days)
6. **Non-Fiction Tie-In: Orchard House** – The Home of Louisa May Alcott and the Setting for <u>Little Women</u> With Compare and Contrast Outline (2-3 days) -- more if you assign an essay from the outline
7. **Opinion Writing** – Did you like the way the first part ended?

End of Part 1 Comprehension Exam	page 57
Exam Answers	page 58
Vocabulary Information	page 59
Vocabulary Assignment	page 60
Vocabulary List 1 for Chapters 1-23	page 62
Vocabulary List 2 for Chapters	page 66
Chapter Comprehension Quizzes Chapters 1-23	page 69
Chapter Comprehension Quiz Answers	page 92
Chapters 1-23 Five Minute to Fluency Chapter Summary Drills	pages 103-125

Version of Little Women I am Using:

Objectives for Teaching Part 1:

Part 1 Teaching Reflections:

Introduction

Little Women, written by Louisa May Alcott, is a coming of age novel, for young women that closely mirrors the life of the author. Alcott was born in November of 1832 in Concord, Massachusetts with transcendentalists, Ralph Waldo Emerson, Nathaniel Hawthorne and Henry David Thoreau as neighbors. Alcott grew up poor but optimistic believing that one could find happiness and spirituality through reason and nature. She, as her transcendentalist neighbors, believed that nonconformity and being true to ones inner-self were the gateway to life and these beliefs are abundantly present throughout the novel.

Little Women seems to be a reflection of Alcott's life. Alcott is personified in the novel's protagonist Jo. Alcott, like Jo is the second of four sisters. Alcott grew up with an older sister, Anna, and two younger sisters Lizzie and Abba May – names very near to the names of the novel's characters – Meg, Beth and Amy. The themes in Alcott's life were also similar to those of the novel: when the Civil War broke out in Alcott's life, she longed to go and fight, she wrote stories to help support her family, her sister Lizzie died at twenty-two from Scarlet Fever, she was a tomboy with an uncontrollable temper and she loved to borrow books from Emerson's large library. Alcott was a suffragette, meaning she fought for women's rights. Her feminist, and again her transcendentalist, beliefs are expressed through the character of Jo March.

Little Women is didactic with an abundance of moral lessons woven through the lives of the March's; however, the story is not preachy, but rather allows readers to learn lessons through the outcome of the story. Lessons include: the power of individuality, the importance of being genuine and the rewards of being good. Oftentimes critics and educators put too much emphasis on what a book is supposed to tell; however, much of literature should be interpreted individually and through the lens of each reader – as it should be with Little Women. There are several overt lessons, but as your students read through the text – make sure they are allows to explore and take away their own lessons and ideas derived from their own experiences!

Little Women tests and obscures gender stereotypes, both male and female. Oftentimes Jo does not want to be a conventional female. In both her desires and her actions, she exasperates conformist gender expectations. For example, she wants to earn a living and does, but this is a duty conventionally reserved for men. Also, she wears a dress with a burn mark to a fancy party, evidence that she does not possess, nor seems to care to possess, a tremendous amount of social grace, a quality that 19th Century American society desired and cultivated in women. Similarly, there are times when Laurie does not want to be a stereotypical man. His greatest desire is to pursue music, at that time a culturally feminine pursuit, instead of business, a culturally masculine pursuit. Even his chosen nickname, Laurie suggests his feminine side. Alcott bestows the highest admiration upon Jo and Laurie, who, in their refusal to embody gender stereotypes, willingly expose themselves to and overcome obstacles.

True to Alcott's transcendental roots, the March sisters seek happiness through daily activities, their dreams, and each other; but when they evade productive work, they end up guilty and remorseful. When they indulge in selfishness by dressing up in the finest cloths, hoard limes, neglect chores, or get revenge, the girls end up unhappy and regretful. The meaningful happiness they find is when they are working, either for a living or for the benefit of their families. The novel validates the imperative nature of the Puritan work ethic, which likens hard work to holiness. This work ethic, in line with the transcendentalist teachings with which Alcott grew up, thrived in New England, where many Puritans lived and where the novel takes place. Alcott conveys the idea that work is not a means to a material end, but rather a means to the expression of inner goodness and creativity through productivity.

Notes: This is a unit for Little Women Part 1 – Which Includes Chapters 1 thru 33 and in some school editions – Part 1 is the entire book. This unit is cross curricular and is Common Core State Standards Aligned. Please look at the Table of Contents and the preview. There are two science activities and several social students and histories activities. The Chapter by Chapter "Think and Writes" are great stand alone assignments or are super for Daily Reading and Writing Warm-Up. Depending on the depth with which you plan to cover this novel – you can also select your favorite "Think and Writes" and add them to the "My Little Women Notebook" packet.

This unit contains chapter by chapter vocabulary for both the standard editions of Little Women and the Hewson Publishing SAT Vocabulary Infused Edition (which is a standard text with SAT word vocabulary substituted for some of the words). It is a really cool edition and contains 255 words footnoted or the Part 1 Hewson Publishing Edition with Common Core State Standards Non-Fiction extras added. Part one is the first 23 chapters. It includes up until Meg's wedding.
- Little Women Part 1: With Extended Readings (Hewson Publishing) ISBN (978-0615803210) or
- Little Women SAT Vocabulary Edition (978-0615800981) – these editions are infused with vocabulary.

Character List:

Josephine March: Jo is the protagonist of Little Women and is the second oldest March sister. The second oldest is the same birth rank as the author had in real life. The author also had one older sister and two younger sisters – just like Jo. Jo has a quick temper and an even quicker tongue. She is an impatient tomboy who wants, above all else, to keep her family happy and together. Jo is somewhat anti-social and refuses to conform. Her ideals are transcendentalist in nature.

Meg March: Meg is the oldest March sister. She is kind and patient and tempers Jo's moods with reasonableness. Meg mothers her sisters and the neighbor-boy Laurie. She is morally virtuous, gentle and loving, but she has a small weakness for luxury that is her burden to bear. As your students read the novel – point out how sometimes Meg tries to change who she is to please others and have students put that into the context of someone they know – or into the context of their own lives.

Beth March: Beth is the third sister by birth. She is quiet and shy and tries to please other people. She is the kindest and most thoughtful. She is almost too good. She is often likened to an angel – which foreshadows her inevitable death. She is almost too good to live in the real world. As the world changes throughout Little Women, Beth is stuck in time and only after she dies can all of the characters change with the world. Beth has anti-social tendencies and is closest to Jo. Beth's one human flaw is she hates housework. She and Jo are alike in that they do not want to live in a world that is gender-divided.

Amy March: Amy is the youngest March sister and is closest to Meg. Both adapt nicely to the world as it exists in the middle of the 1800s. They do not mind their gender roles, but where Meg is generous; Amy is a bit selfish and "petted upon" or spoiled. Amy is an artist, beautiful and understands the art of manipulation. Amy is the foil to Jo – a foil is a character who contrasts with the protagonist in order to highlight the particular qualities of him or her. Amy embraces womanhood – where Jo refuses to submit to the conventions of the day.

Laurie Laurence: Laurie is the orphaned neighbor-boy living with his wealthy grandfather. Laurie is closest to Jo's age and the two are the best of friends. Laurie loves Jo from the beginning; however, his love is unrequited and he ends up marrying Amy. Laurie struggles with who his grandfather wants him to be – mirroring the struggles Jo experiences becoming a lady.

Chapter-by-Chapter Think and Writes

Name: _____ Date: _____

Chapter 1 – Think and Write: Compare and Contrast

Choose one of the March sisters and list her character traits. Then list your character traits. Please use the Venn Diagram below to arrange both sets of character traits in relation to how you and your chosen character are alike and how you are different.

March Sister: _____   Me:
_____   _____
_____   _____
_____   _____
_____   _____
_____   _____
_____   _____

_____   Me

Differences   Similarities   Differences

8

Chapter 1 Active Reading: Making Inferences

> Making an inference is as simple as reading between the lines. It is the same as drawing a conclusion based on what you have read added to your common sense.
>
> Inference = what you read + common sense
>
> You make inferences all of the time. Say you are in a car and you hear a loud crash and glass shattering. You didn't see what happened but you can guess, or infer, that there was a car crash of some kind.
>
> When you read, you make inferences about plot and setting and characters all of the time.
>
> Use the graphic organizer to make inferences about what will happen next.

Character or Event: She was awakened by a shock, so sudden and severe that if Dorothy had not been lying on the soft bed she might have been hurt.	
Details from the Story: Dorothy and her house were swept up in a tornado. The house was flying with the tornado. Dorothy fell asleep as the house took her away on the wind. A shock woke her up and the movement was severe.	**My Experiences:** When I fall I am jerked or feel a severe shock. Like if I am riding my bike and I fall suddenly...I feel a jolt or a shock.
What I can infer: The house landed, probably in a thump. The impact of the crash woke Dorothy up.	

Chapter 1 Making Inferences

Your Turn: Select two events from Chapter 1 and make inferences about what will happen later in the story.

Character or Event:	
Details from the Story:	**My Experiences:**
What I can infer:	

Character or Event:	
Details from the Story:	**My Experiences:**
What I can infer:	

Name: _____ Date: _____

Chapter 2 – Think and Write: Historical Context: Non-Fiction

You read novels for school and for pleasure. You understand plot and setting, but have you ever compared the time a novel is set in to the events going on in the real world during that same time? Think about it. Little Women is set in Concord, Massachusetts during the Civil War. The novel opens in December 1961. The year 1861 was an incredible tumultuous one for the United States, as well as for the March family. Consider that.

In January of 1861 the South seceded from the United States of America. President Lincoln had just been elected President. He was a known opponent of slavery. Seeing this as a threat to their way of life and to their financial stability, the legislature of South Carolina called a convention. The delegates of the convention voted to remove South Carolina from the United States. South Carolina's secession, or break, was followed by the secession of Mississippi, Florida, Alabama, Georgia, Louisiana and Texas. Virginia, Arkansas, Tennessee and North Carolina threatened, but did not secede until a later date.

In February 1861, at another convention, this time in Montgomery Alabama, the seven seceding states created a Confederate Constitution – very similar to that of the United States. They elected Jefferson Davis as president of the Confederate States of America and captured Fort Sumter – all by April.

Soon after the abduction of Fort Sumter, the citizens of Massachusetts heeded President Lincoln's call for troops to put down the rebellion, but to the Little Women, war was just a distant place their father went and served as a minister. Knowing he was in harm's way adds to the drama and power of the close family union in Little Women.

The war was also a place where Jo could not go. In fact, the novel references Jo wanting to go and fight in the war but being allowed to. This information mirrors the author, Louisa May Alcott's, own experience. Louisa, like Jo, wanted to fight in the war but could not because she was female. Woman may not have been allowed to fight, but that does not mean they did not contribute to the war effort. Little Women makes references to making socks for the soldiers among other things. We also know that women served as nurses, spies, maintained their homes and, for the first time in U.S. History, began to work outside the home with regularity to support their families.

In many ways, the Civil War challenged the ideology of the Victorian domesticity that Jo and her sisters struggle with throughout the novel. Before the war, the lives of American women were shaped by a set of ideals about womanhood called "the cult of true womenhood"[1]. Men worked away from home while a woman's role was primarily that of a homemaker. "True women" devoted their lives to the family and home and to creating a comfortable, nurturing environment for their husbands and children.

During the Civil War, women in America began to turn outside of the home. For the first time in American history women played a significant role in a war effort - volunteering in many capacities and serving as Army Nurses and medical aids. Louisa May Alcott was one of the most famous of these Union nurses! The post card above, from the 1860s, is titled Civil War Christmas. It is a Thomas Nast print that tells a story beyond the man and the women who are centered. Look closely at the photos on the post card and think about the chapter of Little Women you just read.

---

[1] *Women in the Civil War*. The History Channel Online. http://www.history.com/topics/women-in-the-civil-war

Think and Write: What do you see as traditional "true womanhood" symbols in the chapter and the post card? What do you see that foreshadows that the role of women is changing? Describe below.

Symbols of "True Womanhood"	
Novel	**Post Card**

Changing Role of Women	
Novel	**Post Card**

Your Narrative regarding the post card versus the novel:

Main Idea: _____

_____

_____

Supporting Detail: _____

_____

_____

_____

_____

Supporting Detail: _____

_____

_____

_____

_____

Supporting Detail: _____

_____

_____

_____

_____

Conclusion: _____

_____

_____

_____

_____

Name: _____ Date: _____

Chapter 3: Write and Think: Critical Thinking

1.   Jo is the tomboy and the least likely of she and Meg to meet someone at the party they attend, but she does. Jo meets Laurie, her neighbor and a boy much like herself. Laurie is fun-loving and mischievous, but appears lonely. Do you agree or disagree? Please explain why or why not -- using details and complete sentences.

_____

_____

_____

_____

_____

_____

_____

_____

_____

2. Please write a paragraph stating who your favorite character is so far and why. Please use details and write in complete sentences.

_____

_____

_____

_____

_____

_____

_____

Name: _____ ____ Date: _____

Chapter 4: Burdens

Chapter 4 reveals much about the characters and their burdens. Please list the character burdens below using complete sentences and lots of detail.

Character	Burdens
Jo	
Meg	
Beth	
Amy	

Name: _____ _____ Date: _____

Chapter 5: Write and Think Active Reading: Character Traits and Motives

Chapters four and five reveal details about the characters. Choose the character from <u>Little Women</u> who is <u>least</u> like you and complete the following exercise.

Instructions: In the space below, please list and the character least like yourself, his or her character traits as well as his or her character motives.

Character Trait: When we talk about a character, we often describe that character in terms of *character traits*. A character trait is a descriptive adjective like *happy or sad* that tells the specific qualities of a character.

Character traits are the kind of words we use to describe ourselves or others. Here you are using the same kind of words to describe fictional characters!

Character Motive: *Character motives* are the reasons behind what characters do. They are the reason for character actions. <u>**They are the reasons why**</u>.

Think in terms of what motivates you. Do you get good grades? Why? What motivates you? Is it to do your best? Is it to play sports? What is your motivation?

Draw Character

Character trait: _____

Character trait: _____

Character trait: _____

Character trait: _____

Character trait: _____

Motive: _____

Motive: _____

Motive: _____

Motive: _____

Motive: _____

Name: _____ Date: _____

Chapter 6: Write and Think: Critical Thinking

Directions: Answer the following questions and then discuss your answers with your partner or neighbor.

1. What is the special bond Mr. Laurence and Beth share? _____
_____
_____
_____
_____

2. What gives Beth the courage to venture over to the Laurence's house? _____
_____
_____
_____
_____

3. Statement: In the absence of her own father, Beth needs a father figure. Please tell whether you agree or disagree with this statement (there is no right or wrong answer) and list the reasons why or why not. _____
_____
_____
_____
_____

Name: _____ Date: _____

Chapter 7: Write and Think: Civil War Critical Thinking

The food Americans ate in the Northeast during the Civil War Era is different than the foods we eat now. Think about it. Have you ever munched on a pickled lime? Have you ever even heard of a pickled lime? I wonder what one would even taste like. The recipe for pickled limes includes: salt, vinegar, red peppers and garlic.

In the space below, please use sensory detail to describe what you think pickled limes would taste like.

_____
_____
_____
_____
_____

Using sensory detail, please talk about the most bizarre food you have ever eaten.

_____
_____
_____
_____
_____
_____
_____
_____

Name: _____ Date: _____

Chapter 8: Write and Think: The Ideal of Womanhood

In Chapter 8, it is revealed that Jo's main weakness is the same as Marmee's: a bad temper. Marmee, however, has learned to control hers through much work and with the help of Mr. March. Jo longs to be like her mother and learn to control her anger and be more like an ideal woman. The 19th Century saw many changes for women and in a very real way the little women convey those changes well.

Think and Write: Read the text in the box. Find one example for each womanly Ideal and site it below:

	The Ideal of Womanhood
_____ _____	During the 1800s it was believed that the ideal of womanhood had essentially four parts--four characteristics any good and proper young woman should cultivate: piety, purity, domesticity, and submissiveness. **Ideal Number One: Piety:** At the time of <u>Little Women</u> Americans believed women were Godly and had more of a tendency towards religion than men. It was also believed that these religious thoughts and tendencies helped women stay righteous and pure. **Ideal Number Two: Purity:** On a similar note female purity was revered. The loss of purity before marriage was unthinkable. Society shunned young women who lost their purity for it was something to be guarded and held sacred. Female purity was also highly revered. Without this purity, a woman was no woman, but rather a lower form of being, a "fallen woman," unworthy of love and unfit for male company. American culture of the early to mid-nineteenth century was obsessed with purity. **Ideal Number Three: Submissiveness** The ideal woman was submissive. Men were supposed to be religious, although not generally. Men were supposed to be pure, although one could not really expect them to be. But men were never supposed to be submissive. Men were to be movers, and doers. Women were to be passive bystanders, submitting to fate, to duty, to God, and to men.

Name: _____ Date: _____

Directions: Read the passage, discuss the topic with your partner and then answer the questions.

Chapter 9: Write and Think: Social Studies

The little women constantly refer to themselves as "poor", only it appears they are poor in relation to the fact that they were previously "rich", not poverty stricken. What they really appear to be is of the emerging middle class.

Historians trace the beginnings of the middle class in America to about the time of the Civil War.[2]

At this time changes occurred. Professions emerged. People who were educated and became doctors and lawyers and professors gained respect. Working and earning money created a boundary between poverty and the upper class. People began to look at life from a broader scope. It wasn't just rich or poor. There was now an in-between

During the time the novel <u>Little Women</u> takes place, America was transitioning into these ideas and the March sisters struggle with their social identity because of the more traditional ways.

Before the Civil War era, one was either rich or poor and much emphasis was placed on whether or not one was born with money. It appears, the only reason the wealthier Moffat, Gardner and other families associate and are friends with the March sisters is because the March family did have money, and therefore social standing, at one time.

But times were changing and those changes are evident in the novel if one looks closely enough.

Making money and education began to be factors toward earning ones way into society and earning respect. Earning into the middle class did not entirely replace the rank of those of born social status – however, the changes were enough so that a value was placed on both earning an education that continues to grow and is evident today.

---

[2] Stuart Blumin, *The Emergence of the Middle Class: Social Experience in the American City, 1760-1900* (Cambridge: Cambridge Univerity Press, 1989), p. 2.

Society was indeed changing and Jo and her sisters were caught up in those changes. And the changes were not small and would alter America forever.

In fact, it could be argued that over the years – earning money and gaining an education replaced being born into certain families or being born with money—as the means to social status – including both the middle and the upper classes. There is now class mobility, the ability to move back and forth between classes – that was not always present.

One example of this class status mobility is evident in how celebrities are treated. Even the poorest person who gains celebrity is seemingly revered by society. At one time, nobility, along with those born wealthy and with proper breeding, were the only people in the "upper class"; today the definition of upper class has shifted to include those who make a lot of money and those who gain celebrity status.

This is true in both America and in other countries.

Likewise, a strong middle class exists today that did not exist before. Doctors and attorneys and teachers and others are now not considered of the lower class. The Marches were workers, but they could read and write and their father was a minister and educator. Today they would be middle class.

During the 19th Century, however, class was still being defined by social rank. The Marches were born into a "good family" so they were defined by character and certain qualities. They referred to themselves as being poor because those around them were rich. But look at the images[3] of the family? Do the Marches appear poor to you? Does it even matter if they are wealthy or poor or if today they would be considered middle class?

Now compare the March family to the Himmel family. Remember, the Himmel family is the truly poor family the March family helps and shares their Christmas breakfast with. Think about how the Hummel family lives in the novel. They don't even have food or clothes. What if the March family compared themselves to the Hummel family rather than the Moffat or Laurence families – would they still consider themselves poor?

Think about these questions, discuss them with a neighbor and then answer the following:

---

[3] Public Domain image from the original text.

Chapter 9: Think and Write Questions

In your own words, define poverty.

What do you know about poverty?

Describe how a poor family lives.

Using your definition, do you think the March family is truly poor?

Name: _____ ____ Date: _____

Chapter 10: Write and Think: The P.C. and the P.O.

The March sisters love to read and form a club, The Pickwick Club, after a book by Charles Dickens. Each girl assumes the identity of a character in the book. It is a private secret club; however, Jo convinces her sisters that Laurie should be allowed to join. In exchange for his admittance, Laurie presents a key for a "Post Office" where the families send letters, flowers and gifts back and forth.

Do you now or have you ever belonged to a club, organization or even a sport's team? Tell about your experiences in the space below. Be sure to include why you joined, what the rules are and what you do in the club or organization or sport's team. If you have never belonged to a club, organization or team make one up like the March girls did!

Club Name:

Purpose:

I joined because…

The rules are…

Other things you should know about it…

Name: _____ Date: _____

Chapter 11: Experiments – Real World Tie-In

Hard work was revered by the emerging middle class in the mid-19th Century. Likewise, many people of the time began to believe that nurturing their inner, spiritual self was more important that paying attention to wealth or money. These people were called transcendentalists and the author of Little Women, Louisa May Alcott, was one of them. Her father was a transcendentalist as well and, some of the most famous transcendentalists ever, were neighbors of the Alcott's including: Ralph Waldo Emerson and Henry David Thoreau.

Transcendentalists wanted only what they deserved and believed what they deserved was directly related to how hard they worked. The March sisters struggle with this notion as they aspire to live it. Even the setting and comparisons to other characters seem to be transcendental ideas. The March's cozy New England home is more desirable than the mansions of their friends. The four sisters lack the money of characters such as Sally Gardner and the Moffat family, but Meg, Jo, Beth and Amy are characterized as being purer and kinder than their wealthy counterparts.

Ideals of transcendentalism include: people will make the right choice if given a chance, materialism is not good and that people should not be dependent on money or belongings.

Think about the passage and answer the following questions:

Please give examples from the book Little Women of "people will make the right choice if given the chance": _____
_____
_____
_____
_____
_____
_____

Please give examples from your life of "people will make the right choice if given the chance": _____
_____
_____
_____
_____
_____
_____

What do you think of the idea that "materialism is not good and people should not be dependent on money or belongings? _____
_____
_____
_____
_____
_____
_____

Name: _____ Date: _____

Chapter 12: Think and Write: Camp Laurence – Your Life

Describe a trip you have been on with your family or friends. Where did you go? What did you do? Did you enjoy it? Why or why not?

Name: _____ Date: _____

Chapter 13: Think and Write

Foreshadowing: As the little women and Laurie are industriously lazing away one of the final days of summer they speak of the Celestial City – meaning heaven. Beth says: "It seems so long to wait, so hard to do. I want to fly away at once, as those swallows fly, and go in at that splendid gate." Her sister tells her if she gets there first to say a good word for her.

What do you suppose a passage such as this would foreshadow? Please be specific and use details.

_____
_____
_____
_____
_____
_____
_____
_____
_____
_____
_____
_____
_____
_____
_____
_____
_____
_____
_____
_____
_____

Name: _____ Date: _____

Chapter 13: Think and Write

Literature and Your Life: What is your Enchanted Castle and what will it take for you to achieve your dream? Please use details and name the character from <u>Little Women</u> whose own Enchanted Castle most emulates your own.

_____
_____
_____
_____
_____
_____
_____
_____
_____
_____
_____
_____
_____
_____
_____
_____
_____
_____
_____
_____
_____

Name: _____ Date: _____

Chapter 14: Think and Write: Your Dreams

What experiences are you getting now that will help with a future dream? Think about something you do now that you would love to get paid for and make a living doing. Write a paragraph about it.

Name: _____ Date: _____

Chapter 15: Think and Write: Questions with Personal Tie-In

1. Discuss the sacrifice Jo made for her family: _____
_____
_____
_____
_____
_____

2. Describe a sacrifice you made for someone. Please include the consequences of this sacrifice: _____
_____
_____
_____
_____
_____

3. Until now Jo has not appeared vain about her physical appearance. What is her source of vanity and why does Meg comfort her? _____
_____
_____
_____
_____

Name: _____ Date: _____

Chapter 16: Think and Write: My Letter to Marmee

Choose your favorite Little Women character and write a letter to Marmee, from her perspective. Include what you are doing at home to help your sisters and the household now that your mother is away.

Date: _____

Dear Marmee:

_____
_____
_____
_____
_____
_____
_____
_____
_____
_____
_____
_____
_____
_____
_____
_____
_____
_____
_____
_____
_____
_____

Love always, _____

Name: _____ Date: _____

Chapter 17: Think and Write: Penicillin

Between 1820 and 1880 there was a world pandemic of scarlet fever. A pandemic is an outbreak or epidemic of a disease over a specific region. For scarlet fever the region was the entire world! Scarlet Fever is a bacterial disease and during the time <u>Little Women</u> is set, people who contracted scarlet fever often died. In 1861, death from scarlet fever was common – today it is uncommon.

In 1887, an English doctor named Edmund Emmanuel Klein identified the cause of scarlet fever: a bacteria known as Streptococcus; however it wasn't until after World War II, well into the 1940s, when penicillin became available as an effective means of curing the disease.

Penicillin is a mold that comes from fungus. It is also a drug that cures certain bacterial infections. There are different types of fungi and each performs a different job. Fungi in soil break down dead plants and animals into nutrients to be reused by other organisms. Fungi is the yeast in bread that makes it rise and fungi is also used to cure diseases. Again, penicillin is a mold first discovered in bread. It is a type of fungi that was eventually found to be an amazing drug!

The discovery of penicillin changed medicine and saved lives.

How did the discovery of penicillin save lives? _____
_____
_____
_____
_____
_____

What do you think Beth contracting scarlet fever foreshadows in the novel Little Women?
_____
_____
_____
_____
_____

Name: _____ Date: _____

Chapter 17 Extension Activity – Science Experiment

1 slice of bread

Water

One plastic zipper baggie

1 piece of graph paper

1. Take a piece of regular bread
2. Trace the outline of the slice of bread on your paper
3. Put a small drop of water on one corner of the bread
4. Seal the bread in a plastic zipper bag
5. Observe your bread over the course of several days – comparing it to the original squares of your graph paper.
6. Count the squares that are covered by the mold each day
7. Record your findings

Day 1 Bread Observation: _____
_____
_____
_____

Day 2 Bread Observation: _____
_____
_____
_____

Day 3 Bread Observation: _____
_____
_____
_____

Create a graph to show the growth of the mold each day.

Name: _____ Date: _____

Chapter 18: Think and Write: My Dark Event

Chapter 18 is titled "Dark Days". Read the quote and think about your own life. Then, in the space provided, please describe a dark thing that has occurred in your life.

How dark the days seemed now, how sad and lonely the house, and how heavy were the hearts of the sisters as they worked and waited, while the shadow of death hovered over the once happy home. Then it was that Margaret, sitting alone with tears dropping often on her work, felt how rich she had been in things more precious than any luxuries money could buy—in love, protection, peace, and health, the real blessings of life. Then it was that Jo, living in the darkened room, with that suffering little sister always before her eyes and that pathetic voice sounding in her ears, learned to see the beauty and the sweetness of Beth's nature, to feel how deep and tender a place she filled in all hearts, and to acknowledge the worth of Beth's unselfish ambition to live for others, and make home happy by that exercise of those simple virtues which all may possess, and which all should love and value more than talent, wealth, or beauty.

Dark Event:	
When it happened:	
Who was involved:	
Details:	
How did this even change you:	
What, if anything did you learn from your dark event:	

34

Name: _____ Date: _____

Chapter 19: Write and Think: Conflict and Graphic Novel Activity

1. What is a conflict of Amy's in this Chapter? _____

_____

_____

_____

2. How would you represent the actions of this chapter using the elements of a graphic novel? Draw pictures to represent a scene from this chapter. Create your own dialogue and illustrations.

35

Name: _____ Date: _____

Chapter 20: Write and Think: Confidential: My Bundle of Naughties

Amy is banished from the March home because she has never had scarlet fever and her family is trying to protect her. Mrs. March returns from nursing the girls' father and visits Amy. Amy is overjoyed to see her mother and Amy tells her mother that she is trying to overcome her "bundle of naughties" – the worst of which are her selfish ways.

In the space below, please describe your own "bundle of naughties", list your worst "naughty" and how you try to overcome it.

My Bundle of Naughties…

My Worst Naughty

How I Overcame My Worst Naughty: _____

36

Name: _____ Date: _____

Chapter 21: Write and Think: Critical Thinking

Laurie's prank hurts Meg. What is Laurie's prank? _____
_____
_____
_____

What is the worst prank you have ever played on someone? _____
_____
_____
_____
_____

It is not revealed how Marmee gets Laurie to apologize and feel bad about his prank. Imagine you are the author of Little Women and write what you would have Marmee say and do to make Laurie sorry for his actions and then to apologize. _____
_____
_____
_____
_____
_____
_____
_____
_____
_____
_____

What is the worst thing you had to apologize for? _____
_____
_____
_____
_____

Name: _____ Date: _____

Chapter 22: Write and Think: What Would My Gift's Be

In Chapter 22, Christmas day arrives again and Mr. March returns home. Think about what you know about each of the March girls and Marmee. Imagine you are a wealthy relative from out of town who visits at Christmas with gifts for all. Thinking of the traits of each character – describe the gift you would give her.

Name: _____ Date: _____

Chapter 23: Write and Think: My Predictions for the Future

As the chapter (and Part 1) ends, the entire extended family is gathered together. Mr. and Mrs. March are reliving their past. Amy is sketching John and Meg, who are sitting together. Beth is lying on the sofa, talking with old Mr. Laurence. Jo is sitting and talking to Laurie, who is leaning on the back of her chair. Predict what is going to happen to each character in Part 2.

Meg	
Jo	
Beth	
Amy	
Laurie	
Marmee	
Father	

My Little Women Notebook

Instructions: Copy one of the following My Little Women Notebook for each student before you begin reading the novel. As you work through the readings and discussions assign the appropriate sections. A guide of when they've been successfully assigned is below; however, it is merely a guide:

8. **Literary Terms**: Throughout the reading.
9. **What is Your Favorite Literary Term and Why** – Halfway through the reading
10. **Write and Think: You and the Novel. Which Character Are You Most Like?** – After Chapter 10
11. **What I Think: Are the Character's Likeable?** – Anytime after Chapter 3 (you may want to include this page twice and have students re-do it at the end of the story and compare to see if their perspective changed).
12. **Social Studies Tie-In: Feminist Literature Non-Fiction Read and Write** – Anytime after Chapter 14 (2-3 days)
13. **Non-Fiction Tie-In: Orchard House** – The Home of Louisa May Alcott and the Setting for Little Women With Compare and Contrast Outline (2-3 days) -- more if you assign an essay from the outline
14. **Opinion Writing** – Did you like the way the first part ended?

You may choose to not assign these lessons as a notebook. I have found that students enjoy packets and like to know what lessons are coming. It helps to walk through all of the lessons and then give students time to look them over. This helps them read with a purpose and makes the individual assignments easier for most students.

The "Think and Writes" from the previous section used to be part of the My Little Women Notebook; however, using them as daily warm-ups or cooperative learning activities enriches even class periods where the novel is not the primary learning focus.

Finally, choose the section of Vocabulary that fits the version of Little Women you are reading. ***Vocabulary List One*** specifically goes with Part 1: Little Women (Hewson Publishing) and Little Women SAT Vocabulary Edition (978-0615800981) – these editions are infused with vocabulary. ***Vocabulary List Two*** goes with all versions.

My **Little Women** Notebook

(Draw Your Cover Above)

Name: _____

Date: _____

Period: _____

Literary Terms

As your class reads the novel and discusses the following literary terms – please write down the definition and a sample from the novel.

allegory	**Definition:** device of using character or story elements to symbolically represent and abstraction in addition to the literal meaning
Example:	
alliteration	**Definition:** repetition of sounds at the beginning of two or more neighboring words
Example:	
allusion	**Definition:** a reference to something that is commonly known – such as a movie or a book or a work of art
Example:	
analogy	**Definition:** comparison or similarity between two different things
Example:	
aphorism	**Definition:** a terse statement which expresses a moral personified
Example:	

Literary Terms Continued

hyperbole	**Definition:** a figure of speech using deliberate overstatement or exaggeration
Example:	
imagery	**Definition:** the sensory details or figurative language used to describe abstractions. This is descriptive language that appeals to sight, hearing, taste, touch or smell
Example:	
verbal irony	**Definition:** Words that literally state the opposite of the speaker's meaning
Example:	
dramatic irony	**Definition:** facts or events that are unknown to a character but the reader or other characters know
Example:	
paradox	**Definition:** a statement that appears to be self-contradictory or opposed to common sense but ends up containing truth or validity
Example:	
foreshadowing:	**Definition:** hints for events that occur later in the reading/storyline
Example:	

Literary Terms Continued

simile:	**Definition:** a comparison of two things or objects using like or as
Example:	
metaphor	**Definition:** a direct comparison not using like or as
Example:	

Think and Write: What is your favorite literary term and why?

_____
_____
_____
_____
_____
_____
_____
_____
_____
_____

Think and Write: You and the Novel

Who is your favorite character from the novel?

Why? Please use detail.

Which character are you most like?

Why? Please use detail.

What I think...

Did you find the characters likable?

I found Meg _____ because _____
_____
_____
_____
_____
_____
_____

I found Jo _____ because _____
_____
_____
_____
_____
_____
_____

I found Beth _____ because _____
_____
_____
_____
_____
_____

I found Amy _____ because _____
_____
_____
_____
_____
_____

I found Laurie _____ because _____
_____
_____
_____
_____
_____

I found Marmee _____ because _____
_____
_____
_____
_____
_____

Choose your favorite quote from the book and write it here: _____
_____
_____
_____

Social Studies Tie-In: Feminist Literature

Think about it. Read the following section and discuss whether you believe that <u>Little Women</u> falls under the category of "feminist literature".

> Feminist literature at the time <u>Little Women</u> was written is based on the definition and principals of feminism. Feminist literature includes all literary works centering on a woman's struggle for equality and to be accepted as a human being. Another aspect of feminist literature is that women are not bound by gender stereotypes. Not all works in this category follow a direct approach towards the goal of equality. What sets apart feminist literature are the characteristics of the feminist movement.
>
> Authors of feminist literature are known to understand and explain the difference between gender and stereotypical gender roles. They believe that while whether a person is a man or a woman is natural and predetermined, society has created the gender a particular perception about gender roles that are not necessarily true. They also believe that gender roles can be altered over time.
>
> The predominance of one gender over the other is a concept that can be seen in almost every society. The fact that this predominance is not in favor of women is an underlying, but blatant, characteristic of feminist literature. Authors in this category argue that any society

Discuss the following questions with your partner or in groups and then write your answers in complete sentences.

What is the role of women in the story? _____
_____
_____
_____
_____
_____
_____

What is the role of the mother character in the story? _____
_____
_____
_____
_____
_____
_____
_____
_____

In your opinion, are the women in the story portrayed as strong and valuable? _____
_____
_____
_____
_____
_____
_____
_____

How are the men portrayed? _____
_____
_____
_____
_____
_____
_____

Non-Fiction Tie-In

Orchard House – The Home of Louisa May Alcott and the Setting for Little Women

The March's home in Little Women is based on the author's home in Concord, Massachusetts. As a young girl, Louisa and her family moved around a lot, but finally settled in Concord in a home named Orchard House.

Orchard House was the place the Alcott's lived in the longest, from 1858 to 1877. At that time the family included Louisa's father, Bronson, her mother (Abigail May), two of her sisters, Anna, May and Louisa. Her sister Elizabeth, whom Beth was modeled after, died a few months before the family moved into the home.

Louisa and her family were vegetarians and grew much of their own food. They believed in women's rights, social reform, abolitionists and held informal theatrical performances – much like the Marches from the novel.

Amy March was modeled after Louisa's sister May. May was the youngest child in the family and a gifted artist.

In 1868, Louisa wrote the novel Little Women in her room on a special folding "shelf" desk built by her father.

Also on the property, to the west of the house, is a structure designed and built by Bronson originally known as "The Hillside Chapel", and later as "The Concord School of Philosophy". The school operated from 1879 to 1888 and was one of the first, and one of the most successful, adult education centers in the country.

Today, visitors can walk through Orchard House and relive the tale of Little Women and get to know the March and Alcott families just a little bit better.

You can take a virtual tour of the Orchard House rooms at: http://www.louisamayalcott.org/rooms.html. Orchard House is large and the property contained an orchard.

Talk it over with your classmates: Think about the poverty Louisa felt she lived in as well as the poverty she wrote about in Little Women. Think about the March family versus the Hummel family and ask yourself, was Louisa, and by extension the March family, poor?

To help you, if time permits, research these questions on the internet.

Setting

Three elements of setting are time, place and environment.

    A. The physical, sensuous world of the work.

    B. The time in which the action of the work takes place.

    C. The social environment of the characters – including the manners, customs, and moral values of the characters' society.

In what time period is Little Women set? _____

Do you think the time period has an impact on the story? Why or why not? _____
_____
_____
_____

Could this story have taken place anywhere but New England in the 1860s? Why or why not?
_____
_____
_____
_____
_____

What part does the environment play in the theme of the novel Little Women?
_____
_____
_____
_____
_____

Non-Fiction: Comparing the Novel to the Lives of the Alcott Family

Published in 1868, Little Women is set in the Alcott family home, Orchard House, in Concord, Massachusetts and is loosely based on Alcott's childhood experiences with her three sisters. The Alcott real life "Little Women" are:

- Anna Bronson Alcott (March 16, 1831 - July 13, 1893)
- Louisa May Alcott (November 29, 1832 - March 6, 1888)
- Elizabeth Sewall Alcott (June 24, 1835 - March 14, 1858)
- May Alcott (March 26, 1840 - December 29, 1879)

The following passage is from Little Women Letters from the House of Alcott by John, S.P. Alcott and published by Little, Brown, and Company (1914), which is currently in the public domain.

CHAPTER VIII

GIRLHOOD AND WOMANHOOD

FAMILIAR to every reader of "Little Women" is the March family's quaint brown house with its many windows, its old-fashioned garden, its homely, homelike air, its unfailing hospitality. This home, as described by Louisa M. Alcott, is a picture of the Alcott home at Concord, the scene of the girlhood and young womanhood of the Alcott children. Many of Louisa's books were written there; "Little Women" was lived there. In Concord,[Pg 141]Anna met John Pratt, and the first love story in "Little Women" is Anna's life romance. There little Beth passed from the material to the spiritual life, and Amy first developed the artistic talents which later caused her work to be sought for by art museums and private collectors.

Anna's marriage was a great trial to Louisa, for from early childhood the two girls had been inseparable companions, and after Anna's marriage Louisa learned to look upon John as her brother.

Louisa's diary in the April following the passing of Elizabeth touches upon the change of homes in Concord, the absence of May, who was studying art in Boston, of Elizabeth and of Anna:

[Pg 142]

April.

Came to occupy one wing of Hawthorne's house (once ours) while the new one was being repaired. Father, mother and I kept house together, May being in Boston, Anna at Pratt farm, & for the first time Lizzy absent. I don't miss her as I expected to do, for she seems nearer & dearer than before,& I am glad to know she is safe from pain & age in some world where her innocent soul must be happy.

Death never seemed terrible to me, & now is beautiful, so I cannot fear it, but find it friendly and wonderful.

Amy's artistic efforts and her failures in "Little Women" are taken from May's actual experiences in Concord. Turning the career of the youngest of the[Pg 143]Alcott girls into a romance earlier in "Little Women" than it actually occurred in life, doubtless prevented Louisa Alcott from chronicling the artistic success of her youngest sister, a success to which she largely contributed and in which she took great pride.

May Alcott's pictures are found to-day in art museums and in leading private collections in this country and abroad. Her copies of Turner are remarkable. In the Kensington Gallery in London students are given them to study in preference to the originals. Several fine examples are in American museums, and a few are owned by members of the Alcott family.

When the Alcotts moved into Orchard[Pg 144]House, the girls painted and papered the interior themselves. May filled the nooks and corners with panels, on which she painted birds and flowers. Over the fireplaces she inscribed mottoes in Old English characters.

The study in Orchard House was the real center of the household. For the chimney piece Ellery Channing wrote an epigram, which May Alcott painted upon it, and which has been used in the stage reproduction of "Little Women":

"The Hills are reared, the Valleys scooped in vain,
If Learning's Altars vanish from the Plain."

In Orchard House to-day, walls, doors, and window casings are etched with May Alcott's drawings, many preserved under[Pg 145]glass, including a miniature portrait of a little girl, naïvely and modestly inscribed "The Artist."

High thoughts and cheerful minds triumphed over poverty in those Concord days. Shortly after the family's return from Fruitlands, Louisa wrote for Ellen Emerson the fairy stories, "Flower Fables." She was at the time only sixteen. This was her earliest published work, and it was many years before she achieved literary fame, although, as did Jo in "Little Women," she materially helped in the support of the family by writing lurid tales.

Literature rather than commerce freed the Alcotts from the burden of debt. Louisa's fame was the result, neither of[Pg 146]accident, nor of a single achievement, but had for its background the whole generous past of her family. Her "Hospital Sketches" were her letters home, when she was serving as hospital nurse during the Civil War. "Little Women" is a chronicle of her family. Louisa certainly made good use of the vicissitudes of the Alcotts. She always saw the funny side and was not afraid to make book material of the home experiences, elevating or humiliating. Her books number between twenty-five and thirty. Nearly every one takes its basic idea from some real experience. The books written by the Alcott family, including some eight or ten published by Mr. Alcott, Louisa's output, and one or[Pg 147]two written by May, fill two shelves of an alcove devoted to Concord authors in the Alcott town library.

(original text, spellings and grammar of passage kept for authenticity).

Assignment:

Compare the events and themes of Little Women with the passage from
<u>Little Women Letters from the House of Alcott.</u>

Compare and Contrast Outline

Purpose:

Factors to look at:

Factors in this Activity	How are the Alike?

Factors in this Activity	How are they Different?

Interpretation or Conclusion:

Developing an Opinion Paragraph

An opinion paragraph states the writer's opinion. A great opinion paragraph includes not only opinions, but facts to support those opinions.

An opinion paragraph:
Asserts the writer's opinion
Explains facts
Makes the reader think
Considers both sides of the argument

Does the story end the way you expected? Why or why not?

Opinion Outline

My Opinion:

Introduction Sentence
Thesis statement:

Sentence 1:

Sentence 2:

Sentence 3:

Concluding Sentence:

Name: _____ **Date:** _____

End of Part 1 Comprehension Exam

1. Name the March daughters from oldest to youngest.

   _____

   _____

   _____

   _____

2. What is the neighbor's name and what is he like? _____
   _____
   _____
   _____

3. Using complete sentences, describe why the girls did not have their large Christmas breakfast. _____
   _____
   _____

4. Which daughter loved to play the piano? _____
5. Who was in love with the neighbor's tutor? _____
6. What sacrifice did Jo give up for her father? _____
7. Who almost died of scarlet fever? _____
8. Using complete sentences, please describe your favorite scene in Part 1:
   _____
   _____
   _____
   _____
   _____
   _____
   _____

Answer to **End of Part 1 Comprehension Exam**

Answers may vary – as long as they fit they are correct.

1. Name the March daughters from oldest to youngest. Meg, Jo, Beth and Amy

2. What is the neighbor's name and what is he like? Laurie Laurence. Laurie is the brother the girls never had. He is fun-loving and seemingly carefree. Laurie is rich and spirited with a kind heart. He is an orphan who lives with his grandfather. He is lonely at first but makes his family with the Marches.

3. Using complete sentences, describe why the girls did not have their large Christmas breakfast. The girls do not have Christmas breakfast because they bring it to a poor family.

4. Which daughter loved to play the piano? Beth

5. Who was in love with the neighbor's tutor? Meg

6. What sacrifice did Jo give up for her father? She cuts her hair – which is her "one beauty"

7. Who almost died of scarlet fever? Beth

8. Using complete sentences, please describe your favorite scene in Part 1: Answers will vary

Vocabulary Information

Vocabulary List 1:

Copy the template and have students use it to copy the vocabulary words from the footnotes of:

- Little Women Part 1: With Extended Readings (Hewson Publishing) ISBN ( ) or
- Little Women SAT Vocabulary Edition (978-0615800981) – these editions are infused with vocabulary.

The words can be used as both vocabulary and spelling words.

Vocabulary List 2:

Copy the template and have students use it to copy the vocabulary words from the attached list. This vocabulary corresponds with any edition of Little Women.

Name: _____ Date: _____

Little Women Chapters _____ Vocabulary

the definitions at the bottom of the novel pages and then write your own sentence containing the word.

	Definition:
	Sentence:
	Definition:
	Sentence:
	Definition:
	Sentence:
	Definition:
	Sentence:
	Definition:
	Sentence:
	Definition:
	Sentence:
	Definition:
	Sentence:
	Definition:
	Sentence:
	Definition:
	Sentence:
	Definition:
	Sentence:

Front side

Vocabulary Continued:

	Definition:	
	Sentence:	
	Definition:	
	Sentence:	
	Definition:	
	Sentence:	
	Definition:	
	Sentence:	
	Definition:	
	Sentence:	
	Definition:	
	Sentence:	
	Definition:	
	Sentence:	
	Definition:	
	Sentence:	
	Definition:	
	Sentence:	
	Definition:	
	Sentence:	

Back side

Vocabulary List 1

Chapter 1
1. Adverse: (adj): feeling repelled, wanting to avoid.
2. Ameliorate: (verb): to make an unpleasant situation better.
3. Appease: (verb): to pacify, calm.
4. Impertinent: (adj): insolent, rude
5. Satirical: (adj): mocking, sarcastic
6. Reproving: (verb): to find fault with
7. Insolent: (adj): rude, disapproving
8. Diatribe: (noun): a critical speech
9. Embellish: (verb): to make more beautiful, to adorn
10. Pervaded: (verb): to permeate, spread throughout
11. Usurped: (verb): to take over by force
12. Innocuous: (adj): harmless, inoffensive
13. Deference: (noun): the act of yielding to one out of respect
14. Convivial: (adj): fond of parties
15. Criteria: (noun): requirements or standards used to make a decision
16. asunder: (adv): apart, divided
17. jubilantly: (adj): filled with joy
18. judicious: (adj): wise, making good decisions
19. jaunty: (adj): lively, perky
20. juncture: (noun): point in time
21. lament: (verb): express sorrow, complain
22. temper: (verb): to bring balance
23. pensive: (adj): thoughtful, reflective

Chapter 2
24. bade: (verb): offer up
25. rummage: (verb): search
26. abashed: (verb): embarrassed, ashamed
27. impetuously: (adj): sudden force of emotion or energy
28. atypical: (adj): odd, not typical
29. extolling: (verb): praising
30. contented: (adj): satisfied, pleased
31. immense: (adj): tremendous, great
32. doublet: (noun): a man's snug-fitting jacket
33. agitation: (noun): worry
34. philter: (noun): charm, potion
35. apparition: (noun): a supernatural appearance
36. reposed: (verb): relaxed, reclined
37. dauntless: (adj): bold, fearless
38. gesticulate: (verb) waves, gestures wildly
39. tumultuous: (adj): wild, noisy
40. rapturous: (adj): elated, enthusiastic
41. acquainted: (adj): to know or get familiar with
42. frolic: (adj): to engage in merrymaking

Chapter 3
43 garret: (noun): attic
44 mortified: (verb): to have caused shame or humiliation
45 blithely: (adj): happily, lighthearted
46 consolingly: (adv): to make feel better
47 petulantly: (adv): sullenly, remorsefully
48 spandy: (adj): neat
49 jovial: (adj): happy, enthusiastic
50 profoundest: (adj): intense
51 appalling: (adj): awful, terrible
52 introversion: (noun): direct one's thoughts inward.
53 gallant: (adj): courteous, smartly
54 beckoned: (verb): call, summon
55 rumpling: (verb): wrinkle, give a crease to
56 rousing: (adj): exciting, stirring

Chapter 4
57 dismally: (adj): dull, cheerless
58 dilapidated: (adj): shabby
59 trudge: (verb): walk slowly and heavily
60 malice: (noun): desire to cause harm
61 penitent: (adj): feeling or showing remorse or sorrow
62 blighted: (verb): spoil or harm
63 discontented: (adj): not satisfied
64 irascible: (adj): made easily angry
65 perilous: (adj): full of danger or risk
66 affliction: (noun): the cause of persistent pain
67 repulsive: (adj): arousing distaste or disgust
68 tempestuous: (adj): characterized by strong emotion
69 ludicrous: (adj): foolish or out of place
70 quenched: (verb): satisfy a desire
71 afflicted: (verb): cause suffering or pain
72 deggerredation: (noun): the act of damaging something
73 harum scarum: (adj): lacking a sense of responsibility
74 gape: (verb): stare with someone's eyes wide open
75 impertinent: (adj): not relevant
76 carnelian: (noun) a semi-precious gemstone that is orange-red
77 mortification: (noun): a feeling of shame
78 diligently: (adv): industriously

Chapter 5
79 mischievous: (adj): playful or naughty in a teasing way
80 betokening: (verb): to give evidence of or to be promising
81 abashed: (verb): to feel embarrassed
82 glowered: (verb): to scowl or have an angry look

Chapter 6
83 indolent: (adj): lazy or idle
84 voraciously: (adj): accessively eager
85 earnest: (adj): serious

86 rapture: (noun): feeling of intense pleasure

Chapter 7
87 personage: (noun): an important person
88 inexorable: (adj): impossible to prevent
89 portentous: (adj): done in an overtly solemnly manner
90 ignominious: (adj): humiliating
91 pensive: (adj): engaged in serious, reflective thought

Chapter 8
92 intricate: (adj): complicated or detailed
93 treacherous: (adj): deceitful
94 disheveled: (adj): unorderly

Chapter 9
95 sumptuously
96 despondency: (noun): low spirits caused by lack of hope
97 dawdled: (verb): waste time, be slow
98 petulantly: (adj): rude behavior
99 alacrity: (noun): brisk and cheerful readiness.
100 languid: (adj): lazy, weak, listless
101 abominable: (adj): worthy of causing distrust or hate

Chapter 10
102 ardent: (adj): devoted
103 convulsed: (verb): uncontrollable movements or of laughter

Chapter 11
104 revel: (verb): to take good pleasure or delight
105 complacently: (adj): casual or indifferent
106 inquisitive: (adv): curious or inquiring
107 apparition: (noun): an unusual or ghostly sight
108 inaudibly: (adj): impossible to hear
109 amiable: (adj): having a pleasant manner

Chapter 12
110 remonstrated: (verb): protested
111 dexterity: (noun): skilled with performing tasks at hand
112 exultation: (noun): Lively or triumphant joy
113 impertinent: (adj): exceeding the limits of good manners
114 fastidious: (adj): attentive
115 lackadaisical: (adj): lacking enthusiasm
116 patronizing: (verb): kindness that betrays superiority

Chapter 13
117 indolent: (adj): lazy or wanting to avoid activity
118 aromatic: (adj): sweet smelling
119 venerable: (adj): given a great deal of respect
120 exploit: (noun): deed or act
121 pique: (noun) wounded pride

Chapter 14
122 promenaded: (verb): rambled or strolled
123 reprovingly: (verb): to find fault with
124 discomfited: (verb): make someone feel embarrassed or uncomfortable
125 condescension: (verb): acting superior
126 countenance: (noun): a facial expression
127 exult: (verb): to rejoice
128 bedewed: (verb): cover

Chapter 15
129 pensively: (adv): suggestive of a sad thought
130 panacea: (adj): all healing

Chapter 16
131 solace: (noun): comfort
132 prudent: (adj): acting with care for the future
133 lamentation: (noun): the act of expressing sorrow
134 forlornly: (adj): feeling sad and pitiful

Chapter 17-13
135 affianced: (verb): engaged to be married
136 incorrigible: (adj): unable to be reformed
137 petulantly: (adj): unreasonably irritable
138 malicious: (adj): intending to do harm
139 disapprobation: (noun): strong disapproval usually on moral grounds
140 contrite: (adj): feeling of remorse or afflicted by guilt
141 pummeled: (verb): strike repeatedly
142 insinuatingly: (adj): provoking doubt or suspicion
143 propitiate: (verb): regain favor
144 irascible: (adj): easily made angry
145 decorous: (adj): keeping polite
146 impracticable: (adj): unworkable
147 peremptorily: (adj): not allowing contradiction
148 tempestuously: (adj): tumultuously or stormy
149 eloquence: (noun): discourse marked by force

Vocabulary List 2

Chapters 1 and 2
1. Knitting: to form fabric from loops of yarn
2. Chaplain: an army minister, pastor, or priest
3. Handkerchiefs: square of cloth used for tissues, or Kleenex
4. Marmee: the Mother's nickname
5. Cologne: perfume
6. Anxious: worried, excited
7. Embroidered: sewn with decorative stitches
8. Pitiful: sad, pathetic
9. Intentions: what someone means to do

Chapters 3-5
10. Fussed: taken extra care with, sometimes too much care
11. Gala: fancy event
12. Maroon: dark red, burgundy
13. Chrysanthemum: a type of flower; often called a mum
14. "Out of sorts": not quite right, out of control
15. Governess: a person hired to teach and take care of children
16. Confide: to share
17. Stately: proud, intimidating
18. Conservatory: a room, or building made of mostly glass used to grow flowers in, greenhouse

Chapters 6-8
19. Stern: firm, somewhat angry
20. Fib: a lie
21. Putting on airs": acting like a snob
22. Fiancé: a person engaged to be married
23. Society: the social life of wealthy, important, and fashionable people
24. Train: a long part of a dress that trails on the ground behind a woman
25. Champagne: sparkling wine
26. Spectacle: to behave foolishly in front of people
27. Rubbish: worthless, trash
28. Parlor: a formal room like a fancy living room
29. Asparagus: skinny green vegetable with a pointy top
30. Mortified: very embarrassed
31. Gales: loud outburst of laughter

Chapters 9-11
32. Croquet: a game played using mallets to knock wooden balls through metal arches
33. Manuscript: a written out story or article
34. Mischief: trouble
35. " 'fess up": confess
36. Telegram: a message sent by telegraph between distant places
37. Rash: foolish, without thinking
38. Selflessness: not thinking of your own needs
39. Stifled: covered up

40 Vain: being too proud about how you look

Chapters 12-14
41 Scarlet fever: a contagious disease, often deadly, that included a red rash on the skin
42 Grocer: one who sells groceries
43 Hovered: to wait near by, hanging over
44 Ordeal: difficult time, challenge
45 Turquoise: blue-green stone
46 Invalids: sick or injured people who cannot move around easily
47 Ceremoniously: formally
48 Stammered: stuttered
49 Sentiments: sweet thoughts

Chapters 15-17
50 Twilight: sunset
51 Delicate: fragile, easily broken
52 Dovecote: a birdhouse
53 Promenading: walking
54 Bittersweet: both bitter and sweet, both happy and sad
55 Charcoal: black drawing pencil
56 Plaster casts: molds made of plaster
57 Submit: to give in
58 Domestic: having to do with things at home
59 Preserves: jams and jellies
60 Currant: a small sour berry
61 Demi: prefix meaning half

Chapters 18-20
62 Haughty: stuck up
63 Sociable: enjoying peoples' company
64 Dismay: to be upset, hopeless
65 "Favors burden you": a phrase that meant a person did not want others to do things for him or her
66 because then he or she felt that one must do something nice back
67 Stout: large, sturdy
68 "Going abroad": traveling to a foreign country

Chapters 21-23
69 Immensely: not able to be measured
70 Accomplished: having done many things well
71 Transparent: somewhat see-through
72 Escorting: going along with
73 Regret: wishing things were different

Chapters 24-26
74 Wearied: extremely tired
75 Despair: without hope
76 Content: satisfied, happy
77 Relics: old items left from long ago

Chapters 27-28
78 Trooped: walking purposefully
79 Cordially: politely
80 Cross: angry, upset
81 Coolly: uninterested, bored

Name: _____ Date: _____

Chapter One: Comprehension Quiz

1. Why does Meg say their mother suggested there be no presents for Christmas this year?

2. What does Jo fret about having to do to earn money?

3. Meg calls Jo tomboy and Amy a goose. What does she call Beth?

4. Describe Meg.

5. What song do they sing that has become a household custom?

6. Summarize the chapter you just read.

_____
_____
_____
_____
_____
_____
_____
_____
_____
_____

Name: _____ Date: _____

Chapter Two: Comprehension Quiz

1. Who woke up first on Christmas morning?

2. What surprise do the girls have for their mother?

3. What does mother suggest the family do with their Christmas breakfast?

4. Since no males were permitted, who plays the male parts in the play?

5. Who brought over the Christmas dinner feast?

6. How did the Laurence boy's grandfather find out the Marches gave up their Christmas breakfast?

7. Use details to describe your favorite part of this Chapter.

Name: _____ Date: _____

Chapter Three: Comprehension Quiz

1. Where do Meg and Jo get to dress up and go?

2. Which sister has soiled gloves?

3. At the New Year's Eve part, why doesn't Jo talk with the girls and dance with Meg?

4. Who does Jo meet and talk with at the dance?

5. What happens to Meg at the dance so that she can't walk home?

6. Summarize the chapter you just read.

_____
_____
_____
_____
_____
_____
_____
_____
_____
_____
_____
_____

Name: _____ Date: _____

Chapter Four: Comprehension Quiz

1. In this chapter it is revealed how Mr. March lost his fortune.

2. What kind of person is Beth?

3. What is Amy's talent?

4. How does Marmee teach the girls to stop wishing for things they don't have?

5. Why does Jo suit Aunt March?

6. What is Beth too bashful to do?

7. Summarize the chapter you just read.

_____
_____
_____
_____
_____
_____
_____
_____

Name: _____ Date: _____

Chapter Five: Comprehension Quiz

1. What does Jo do when she discovers that Laurie is sick and must stay home?

2. Does Mr. Laurence like Laurie playing the piano?

3. Why then does Mr. Laurence like Beth playing the piano?

4. Why does Jo say she doesn't go to school?

5. Where does Laurie leave Jo to wait when he must go to see the doctor?

6. Summarize the chapter you just read.

_____
_____
_____
_____
_____
_____
_____
_____
_____
_____
_____
_____
_____
_____

Name: _____ Date: _____

Chapter Six: Comprehension Quiz

1. Beth is shy and yet she warms up to Mr. Laurence. Why?

2. How long did Beth stay at the Laurence playing the piano?

3. What does Beth decide to do for Mr. Laurence to express her gratitude?

4. What does Mr. Laurence give to Beth after he receives the slippers?

5. What uncharacteristic move did Beth do to thank Mr. Laurence for the piano?

6. Summarize the chapter you just read.

_____
_____
_____
_____
_____
_____
_____
_____
_____
_____
_____
_____

Name: _____ Date: _____

Chapter Seven: Comprehension Quiz

1. Why is Amy "in debt" at school?

2. Who gives Amy the money to buy limes?

3. What happens to the limes at school?

4. Does Amy have to go back to school?

5. Summarize the chapter you just read.

_____
_____
_____
_____
_____
_____
_____
_____
_____
_____
_____

Name: _____ Date: _____

Chapter Eight: Comprehension Quiz

1. Where does Laurie take Meg and Jo?

2. Which sister wants to go but Jo says no?

3. What does Amy do because she is angry with Jo?

4. What does Marmee tell Jo regarding her anger?

5. What does Jo want to do to feel better?

6. What happens when they are skating?

7. What is your favorite part of this chapter?

_____
_____
_____
_____
_____
_____
_____
_____

Name: _____ Date: _____

Chapter Nine: Comprehension Quiz

1. Who does Meg get to go with for a fortnight of fun?

2. What does mother give Meg out of the treasure box?

3. What does Meg bring to wear for the party?

4. How did Meg feel about being home after her adventure with her friends?

5. Who didn't like the way Meg was dressed up and how she behaved at the party?

6. Summarize the chapter you just read.
_____
_____
_____
_____
_____
_____
_____
_____
_____

Name: _____ Date: _____

Chapter Ten: Comprehension Quiz

1. What is the Pickwick Club?

2. What does Laurie do in exchange for being a member of the club?

3. What is the club's newspaper called?

4. Name all five members of the Pickwick Club – their real names.

5. What is the last name of the little women?

6. Summarize the chapter you just read.

_____
_____
_____
_____
_____
_____
_____
_____

Name: _____ Date: _____

Chapter Eleven: Comprehension Quiz

1. What is the experiment?

2. What happens to Beth's bird?

3. When Mrs. March asks the girls if they are satisfied with their experiment, what do they reply?

4. What lesson has Mrs. March taught the girls?

5. What does Jo decide her summer holiday task is to be?

6. Summarize the chapter you just read.

_____
_____
_____
_____
_____
_____
_____
_____

Name: _____ Date: _____

Chapter Twelve: Comprehension Quiz

1. Who is post-mistress of their little post office?

2. What is at the post office for Meg?

3. What does Marmee's letter to Jo say?

4. What does Laurie write to Jo?

5. What annoys Jo when they are playing croquet?

6. Summarize the chapter you just read.

_____
_____
_____
_____
_____
_____
_____
_____

Name: _____ Date: _____

Chapter Thirteen: Comprehension Quiz

1. What is Laurie doing when he sees the girls walking by?

2. What are the girls doing?

3. Why do they do their work out of doors?

4. What does Beth say she would like for her Castle in the Air?

5. What does Amy want for her Castle in the Air?

6. Summarize the chapter you just read.

_____
_____
_____
_____
_____
_____
_____
_____

Name: _____ Date: _____

Chapter Fourteen: Comprehension Quiz

1. What does Jo bring to town?

2. What secret does Laurie tell Jo?

3. What does Laurie suggest to cheer up Jo?

4. Who do Laurie and Jo meet at the bottom of the hill?

5. Does Jo get paid for her first stories?

6. Summarize the chapter you just read.

_____
_____
_____
_____
_____
_____
_____
_____

Name: _____ Date: _____

Chapter Fifteen: Comprehension Quiz

1. What does Meg think about November?

2. What does the telegram that Marmee receive say?

3. Who does Marmee turn to for money?

4. Who goes as Marmee's travel companion?

5. What does Jo sacrifice to earn money for her father?

6. Summarize the chapter you just read.

_____
_____
_____
_____
_____
_____
_____
_____
_____

Name: _____ Date: _____

Chapter Sixteen: Comprehension Quiz

1. How do the girls communicate with their mother?

2. What does Hannah give the girls to drink as a treat?

3. In one of Jo's letters she includes a poem. What is the poem about?

4. What does Laurie's grandfather offer in his letter?

5. Which character does not have a letter represented in Chapter Sixteen?

6. Summarize the chapter you just read.

_____
_____
_____
_____
_____
_____
_____
_____
_____

Name: _____ Date: _____

Chapter Seventeen: Comprehension Quiz

1. Why do the girls relax their diligence to their chores?

2. Marmee asks all of the girls to check in on the Himmel's every day. Who is the only girl who does?

3. What happens one day to traumatize Beth?

4. What illness does Beth contract?

5. Who is sent away because she has never had scarlet fever?

6. Summarize the chapter you just read.

_____
_____
_____
_____
_____
_____
_____
_____
_____

Name: _____ Date: _____

Chapter Eighteen: Comprehension Quiz

1. Who telegrams for Marmee first?

2. Who does Amy befriend at Aunt Marches?

3. What does Esther say Amy will receive from her aunt?

4. What do Amy and Esther set up in a closet?

5. What does Amy create in case she falls ill?

6. Summarize the chapter you just read.

_____
_____
_____
_____
_____
_____
_____
_____

Name: _____ Date: _____

Chapter Twenty: Comprehension Quiz

1. Who goes to visit Amy to tell her Beth is getting better?

2. Who surprises Amy because she has returned?

3. Who does Marmee talk to about Meg and Mr. Brooke?

4. How old does Marmee think Meg should be before she gets married?

5. Does Marmee think Meg loves John Brooke?

6. Summarize the chapter you just read.
_____
_____
_____
_____
_____
_____
_____
_____
_____

Name: _____ Date: _____

Chapter Twenty-One: Comprehension Quiz

1. Who pranks Meg with a false letter from John?

2. Who does Laurie promise he will not tell about the prank?

3. How does Laurie's prank make Meg feel?

4. Who gets Laurie's grandfather to apologize?

5. What does Jo find at the end of the chapter?

6. Summarize the chapter you just read.

_____
_____
_____
_____
_____
_____
_____
_____

Name: _____ Date: _____

Chapter Twenty-Two: Comprehension Quiz

1. What do Laurie and Jo do for Beth?

2. Who comes to surprise the Marches?

3. Who arranged for the surprise?

4. Why is Jo upset?

5. What does Beth do at the end of the chapter that she has not done for a long time?

8. Summarize the chapter you just read.

_____
_____
_____
_____
_____
_____
_____
_____

Name: _____ Date: _____

Chapter Twenty-Three: Comprehension Quiz

1. How old does Meg reveal Jo is?

2. Does Meg like Mr. Brooke?

3. What doe Mr. Brooke say he came to get?

4. Who couldn't resist her longing to see her nephew?

5. What pushes Meg to declare that she will be with Mr. Brooke?

6. Summarize the chapter you just read.

_____
_____
_____
_____
_____
_____
_____
_____

Quiz Answers

Name: _____ Date: _____

Chapter One: Comprehension Quiz

1. Why does Meg say their mother suggested there be no presents for Christmas this year? Because it was going to be a hard winter and their money thinks that money should not be spent on pleasures when soldiers are suffering in the army.

2. What does Jo fret about having to do to earn money? Jo frets about having to be shut up for hours with a fussy and nervous old lady.

3. Meg calls Jo tomboy and Amy a goose. What does she call Beth? She calls Beth a dear and nothing more.

4. Describe Meg. Meg is the eldest of the four girls. She is 16 and is pretty, plump and fiar with large eyes and plenty of soft brown hair.

5. What song do they sing that has become a household custom? "Crinkle, Crinkle Little Tar" or Twinkle, Twinkle Little Star.

Name: _____ Date: _____

Chapter Two: Comprehension Quiz

1. Who woke up first on Christmas morning? Jo woke up first on Christmas morning.

2. What surprise do the girls have for their mother? They used their money to buy her gifts.

3. What does mother suggest the family do with their Christmas breakfast? She suggests they give it to the poor family.

4. Since no males were permitted, who plays the male parts in the play? Jo plays the male parts in the play.

5. Who brought over the Christmas dinner feast?   The Laurence boy's grandfather.

6. How did the Laurence boy's grandfather find out the Marches gave up their Christmas breakfast? Hannah told one of his servants and this pleased him.

Name: _____ Date: _____

Chapter Three: Comprehension Quiz

1. Where do Meg and Jo get to dress up and go? A New Year's ball/dance.

2. Which sister has soiled gloves? Jo has soiled gloves.

3. At the New Year's Eve part, why doesn't Jo talk with the girls and dance with Meg? She is shy.

4. Who does Jo meet and talk with at the dance? Their neighbor Laurie Laurence.

5. What happens to Meg at the dance so that she can't walk home? Meg sprains her ankle.

Name: _____ Date: _____

Chapter Four: Comprehension Quiz

1. In this chapter it is revealed how Mr. March lost his fortune. How did it happen? Mr. March lost his fortune helping an unfortunate friend.

2. What kind of person is Beth? Beth is kind and compassionate.

3. What is Amy's talent? Amy is an artist.

4. How does Marmee teach the girls to stop wishing for things they don't have? Marmee tells them stories that reference how they have been behaving.

5. Why does Jo suit Aunt March? Aunt March is lame and needed an active person to wait upon her.

6. What is Beth too bashful to do? Beth is too bashful to go to school.

Name: _____ Date: _____

Chapter Five: Comprehension Quiz

1. What does Jo do when she discovers that Laurie is sick and must stay home? She visits him.

2. Does Mr. Laurence like Laurie playing the piano? No, it reminds him of Laurie's mother and Mr. Laurence didn't care for her.

3. Why then does Mr. Laurence like Beth playing the piano? His granddaughter used to play the piano and she died.

4. Why does Jo say she doesn't go to school? Jo says she doesn't go to school because she is a business women.

5. Where does Laurie leave Jo to wait when he must go to see the doctor? She waits in the library.

Name: _____ Date: _____

Chapter Six: Comprehension Quiz

1. Beth is shy and yet she warms up to Mr. Laurence. Why? Mr. Laurence has a piano and Beth loves to play.

2. How long did Beth stay at the Laurence playing the piano? Beth played until Hannah came to take her home to dinner.

3. What does Beth decide to do for Mr. Laurence to express her gratitude? Beth decides to make him a pair of slippers.

4. What does Mr. Laurence give to Beth after he receives the slippers? Mr. Laurence gives Beth a cabinet piano.

5. What uncharacteristic move did Beth do to thank Mr. Laurence for the piano? Beth hugged and kissed him.

Name: _____ Date: _____

Chapter Seven: Comprehension Quiz

1. Why is Amy "in debt" at school? The girls give each other pickled limes and she has not done so.

2. Who gives Amy the money to buy limes? Her sister Meg gives Amy the money to buy limes.

3. What happens to the limes at school? The limes are against the rules and Amy's teacher has them tossed out of the window.

4. Does Amy have to go back to school? No not until her father comes home and finds her a new school.

Name: _____ Date: _____

Chapter Eight: Comprehension Quiz

1. Where is Laurie taking Meg and Jo? He is taking them to see "Seven Castles".

2. Which sister wants to go but Jo says no? Amy wants to go.

3. What does Amy do because she is angry with Jo? She burns the book of stories Jo is writing.

4. What does Marmee tell Jo regarding her anger? Don't let the sun go down on your anger.

5. What does Jo want to do to feel better? She asks Laurie to go skating with her.

6. What happens when they are skating? Amy falls through the ice and Laurie has to rescue her.

Name: _____ Date: _____

Chapter Nine: Comprehension Quiz

1. Who does Meg get to go with for a fortnight of fun? She is going on vacation with Annie Moffat.

2. What does mother give Meg out of the treasure box? Mother gives Amy silk stockings, the pretty carved fan and a lovely blue sash.

3. What does Meg bring to wear for the party? She is bringing her tarlatan.

4. How did Meg feel about being home after her adventure with her friends? She was grateful to be home.

5. Who didn't like the way Meg was dressed up and how she behaved at the party? Her friend and neighbor Laurie.

Name: _____ Date: _____

Chapter Ten: Comprehension Quiz

1. What is the Pickwick Club? The Pickwick Club is a secret club that the girls invent. It is a literary club based on a book by Charles Dickens.

2. What does Laurie do in exchange for being a member of the club? Laurie gives a key to a play mailbox he set up between their houses.

3. What is the club's newspaper called? The club's newspaper is called the Pickwick Portfolio.

4. Name all five members of the Pickwick Club – their real names. Meg, Jo, Beth, Amy and Laurie.

5. What is the last name of the little women? Their last name is March

Name: _____ Date: _____

Chapter Eleven: Comprehension Quiz

1. What is the experiment? To do nothing for a week of summer to see if they enjoyed it.

2. What happens to Beth's bird? In not doing any work for a week she neglected Pip and he died.

3. When Mrs. March asks the girls if they are satisfied with their experiment, what do they reply? Yes they are satisfied.

4. What lesson has Mrs. March taught the girls? The importance of doing at least a little work.

5. What does Jo decide her summer holiday task is to be? Jo's holiday task is that she is going to learn to cook.

Name: _____ Date: _____

Chapter Twelve: Comprehension Quiz

1. Who is post-mistress of their little post office? Beth is post-mistress of their little post office.

2. What is at the post office for Meg? One of her gloves.

3. What does Marmee's letter to Jo say? That she is proud of the efforts Jo is making to control her temper.

4. What does Laurie write to Jo? That some English boys and girls are going to join them and they are going to pitch a tent, have a fire and make messes. He invites every one to come.

5. What annoys Jo when they are playing croquet? Fred cheats and then says he didn't.

Name: _____ Date: _____

Chapter Thirteen: Comprehension Quiz

1. What is Laurie doing when he sees the girls walking by? Laurie is laying on a hammock.

2. What are the girls doing? Tasks for the Busy Bee Society.

3. Why do they do their work out of doors? Their mother likes them to be outside as much as possible and to be industrious, so they bring things to do outside.

4. What does Beth say she would like for her Castle in the Air? She says that since she has her piano she has everything she wants. She just now wishes they would all stay together forever.

5. What does Amy want for her Castle in the Air? Amy wants to be a famous artist.

Name: _____ Date: _____

Chapter Fourteen: Comprehension Quiz

1. What does Jo bring to town? Jo brings stories for the newspaperman to town.

2. What secret does Laurie tell Jo? Laurie tells Jo that Mr. Brooke kept on of Meg's gloves and he carries it around with him.

3. What does Laurie suggest to cheer up Jo? Laurie suggests that they run down the hill.

4. Who do Laurie and Jo meet at the bottom of the hill? Laurie and Jo meet Meg at the bottom of the hill.

5. Does Jo get paid for her first stories? No, but she is told she will for future stories.

Name: _____ Date: _____

Chapter Fifteen: Comprehension Quiz

1. What does Meg think about November? That it is the most disagreeable month out of the entire year.

2. What does the telegram that Marmee receive say? The telegram says that Mr. March is ill and she must come to Washington, D.C.

3. Who does Marmee turn to for money? Marmee sends Laurie to Aunt March for money.

4. Who goes as Marmee's travel companion? John Brooks, Laurie's tutor, accompanies Mrs. March to Washington, D.C.

5. What does Jo sacrifice to earn money for her father? Jo cuts what Amy calls Jo's "one beauty" her hair.

Name: _____ Date: _____

Chapter Sixteen: Comprehension Quiz

1. How do the girls communicate with their mother? They communicate by letter.

2. What does Hannah give the girls to drink as a treat? Hannah makes and gives the girls coffee as a treat.

3. In one of Jo's letters she includes a poem. What is the poem about? Washing day, A Song from the Suds being its title.

4. What does Laurie's grandfather offer in his letter? Money if Marmee needs it for anything.

5. Which character does not have a letter represented in Chapter Sixteen? Hannah does not have a letter represented (neither does Father, etc.)

Name: _____ Date: _____

Chapter Seventeen: Comprehension Quiz

1. Why do the girls relax their diligence to their chores? They feel better because they have word that their father is mending.

2. Marmee asks all of the girls to check in on the Himmel family every day. Who is the only girl who does? Beth is the only girl who checks in on the Himmel family each day.

3. What happens one day to traumatize Beth? One of the Himmel's babies dies in her arms.

4. What illness does Beth contract? Beth catches scarlet fever.

5. Who is sent away because she has never had scarlet fever? Amy is sent away because she has never had scarlet fever.

Name: _____ Date: _____

Chapter Eighteen: Comprehension Quiz

1. Who telegrams for Marmee first? Laurie telegrams for Marmee.

2. Who does Amy befriend at Aunt Marches? Amy befriends Esther the servant.

3. What does Esther say Amy will receive from her aunt? Her turquoise ring.

4. What do Amy and Esther set up in a closet? They set up a chapel for Amy to pray.

5. What does Amy create in case she falls ill? Amy writes up a will in case she falls ill.

Name: _____ Date: _____

Chapter Twenty: Comprehension Quiz

1. Who goes to visit Amy to tell her Beth is getting better? Laurie goes to visit Amy.

2. Who surprises Amy because she has returned? Marmee surprises Amy.

3. Who does Marmee talk to about Meg and Mr. Brookes? Marmee talks to Jo.

4. How old does Marmee think Meg should be before she gets married? Marmee thinks Meg should be twenty before she leaves the house.

5. Does Marmee think Meg loves John Brooke? No, she thinks she does not love him yet, but that she will soon learn to.

Name: _____ Date: _____

Chapter Twenty-One: Comprehension Quiz

1. Who pranks Meg with a false letter from John? Laurie pranks Meg.

2. Who does Laurie promise he will not tell about the prank? He promises Marmee

3. How does Laurie's prank make Meg feel? Embarrassed

4. Who gets Laurie's grandfather to apologize? Jo gets Laurie's grandfather to apologize.

5. What does Jo find at the end of the chapter? Jo finds a bit of paper scribbled over with the words, "Mrs. John Brooke."

Name: _____ Date: _____

Chapter Twenty-Two: Comprehension Quiz

1. What do Laurie and Jo do for Beth? They make a snowman?

2. Who comes to surprise the Marches? Father comes home.

3. Who arranged for the surprise? Mr. Laurence arranged for the surprise.

4. Why is Jo upset? Jo is upset because she feels Meg is slipping away.

5. What does Beth do at the end of the chapter that she has not done for a long time? She plays the piano.

Name: _____ Date: _____

Chapter Twenty-Three: Comprehension Quiz

1. How old does Meg reveal Jo is? Jo is sixteen.

2. Does Meg like Mr. Brooke? Yes, Meg likes Mr. Brooke.

3. What doe Mr. Brooke say he came to get? Mr. Brooke goes to the Marches to get his umbrella.

4. Who couldn't resist her longing to see her nephew? Aunt March wanted to see father.

5. What pushes Meg to declare that she will be with Mr. Brooke? Aunt March's tirade

Five Minutes to Fluency

Instructions

Fluency Practice is essential for all readers – especially with those struggling to read at grade level. The following drills are designed to be read in pairs, with the stronger reader reading first. They are great practice for all students and a quick way to fit RTI for fluency in a busy day.

Properly training students how to complete the Five Minutes to Fluency drills will ensure that the activity runs smoothly. The most important thing to do is model the program on day one.

Explain the following as you are modeling

Procedure:

- Copy and distribute the Sample Passage
- Make a transparency of the Sample Passage or scan and project it for the class to see
- Pair students up with fluency partners
- Choose a partner and have him or her read the passage
- Put his or her name on your paper and explain that you students will do this as well
- Put a line over each word the student gets wrong
- Model how to calculate the cwpd by counting the total number of words read and then subtract the errors.

Name: _____   Date: _____

Fluency – Chapter 1 (4.4)

This is a one-minute timed reading. When time is up calculate the total CWPM read by using the formula at the bottom of the page.

Chapter 1 is titled *Playing Pilgrims*. In this chapter the main characters are	13
introduced. They are four sisters: Meg, Jo, Beth, and Amy. The girls are	26
trying to decide what to get each other for Christmas. This year their father	40
is away at war and funds are limited. They complain a bit. They finally	54
decide that they will each buy a gift for Marmee instead of a gift for	69
themselves.	70
The reader learns that the March family used to be wealthy, but that it	84
isn't anymore. They talk about the play they are going to do for Christmas.	98
Then their mother comes home with a letter from father. Their father is a	112
Union soldier in the Civil War. His letter reminds the girls to be good. This	127
makes the girls feel bad about their earlier complaining. They talk and think	140
about their burdens. Meg is the oldest sister. Her burden is her vanity. Jo,	154
the second sister's burden is her temper. Beth's burden is her dislike of	167
housework and Amy's is her selfishness. Their burdens foreshadow events	177
that will happen later in the story	184
To help with their burdens, Marmee suggests they play pilgrims. It is a	197
game the girls' played when they were younger. They agree to play the game	211
again. The game will help them put value on what is important and help	225
them live past their burdens.	231
They gather together and sing before bedtime.	238
Chapter One shows how close the family is. It also shows how much they	251
value each other and how good they are towards one another. Their	263
goodness is reflected in the characters and in the kindness they show toward	276
one another.	278

Total Words Read: _____
Minus errors: _____
= CWPM   _____

Name: _____   Date: _____

Fluency – Chapter 2 (3.5)

This is a one-minute timed reading. When time is up calculate the total CWPM read by using the formula at the bottom of the page.

Chapter 2 is titled *A Merry Christmas*. The girls wake up to find their	14
mother has placed a book under each of their pillows. It is a copy of the	29
Pilgrim's Progress. They each vow to read from it every day.	40
Meg goes downstairs to find her mother. Hannah, their maid, tells her	52
that Marmee is not home. Hannah tells Meg that Marmee has gone to help	66
their poor neighbors.	69
When Marmee returns she asks the girls if they will give up their	82
delicious breakfast and give it to their neighbors instead. They bundle up	94
the food and take it to their neighbors. The poor family lives in a shack.	109
There is a mother and seven children. One is a newborn. They are German	123
immigrants. They are thankful for the food.	130
The girls and their mother go home and eat bread and milk. They are	144
happy that they shared their feast. Marmee leaves to gather clothes for the	157
poor family. When she returns the girls present her with their gifts. She is	171
happy.	172
Meg, Jo, Beth and Amy spend the rest of the day preparing for their play.	187
Many of their friends come over that evening and watch the play. A few	201
things go wrong, but the audience loves the play. After their guests leave,	214
Hannah tells the family it is time to eat. They enter the dining room and	229
there is a feast with food and cake and fancy fruit and candy. They discover	244
what their old neighbor, Mr. Laurence brought the food. Marmee tells the	256
girls that Mr. Laurence sent over the gift of their dinner because they were so	271
charitable that morning.	274
The girls talk about the Laurence family. They talk about Mr. Laurence	286
and his grandson, Laurie. Laurie studies hard with a tutor.	296
At the end of the chapter their father is mentioned. Beth wants to send	310
him some of the flowers Mr. Laurence gave them.	319

Total Words Read: _____
Minus errors: _____
= CWPM _____

Name: _____   Date: _____

Fluency – Chapter 3 (2.2)

This is a one-minute timed reading. When time is up calculate the total CWPM read by using the formula at the bottom of the page.

Chapter 3 is titled *The Laurence Boy*. Jo is in the attic. She is reading a	16
book and eating apples. Meg shows Jo an invitation to a New Year's Eve	30
dance. It is at the Gardner's home. The girls talk about what they will wear.	45
They each have one nice dress, but the dresses are made of cotton. Their	60
friends will be wearing silk.	65
Jo is a tomboy and doesn't keep her clothes very nice. Meg's are kept in	80
perfect condition. Jo's one good dress has a burn mark in the back. Jo has	95
also ruined her gloves. Meg insists that Joe wear them. They decide that	108
each girl should wear one of Meg's good gloves and carry one of Jo's stained	123
ones.	124
The next evening the girls get ready for the party. Amy does Meg's hair,	138
but accidently burns it. Amy ties one of her best ribbons on it to hide the	153
burns.	154
The girls arrive at the party. They are greeted by Mrs. Gardiner and her	167
six daughters. Meg is very good friends with Sallie Gardiner. Meg goes off	180
and immediately has a good time. Jo stays back. She feels awkward and	193
stays against the wall to hide her burn spots. Meg dances and Jo ducks	207
behind a curtain. The curtain is already taken. The Laurence boy, Laurie,	219
from next door, is there. Jo wants to run away, but Laurie will not let her.	235
They have a great time talking and eating.	243
Jo and Laurie dance. They sit on the stairs to rest. Meg limps over to	258
them. She has sprained her ankle on her high shoes. Laurie gets them	271
dessert. Hannah comes to pick them up. Meg can't walk. Laurie offers them	284
his carriage and he escorts them home.	291
The girls arrive home. Jo has brought her sisters some treats from the	304
party. Meg thinks it is rude, but they talk about what a fine time they had.	320

Total Words Read: _____
Minus errors: _____
= CWPM _____

Name: _____   Date: _____

Fluency – Chapter 4 (4.6)

This is a one-minute timed reading. When time is up calculate the total CWPM read by using the formula at the bottom of the page.

Chapter 4 is titled *Burdens*. The holidays are over. It is the day after the party. Meg is depressed. Jo tries to make her feel better. They go down to breakfast and everyone is in a bad mood. Even though Hannah is in a bad mood as well, she remembers to make Meg and Jo's turnovers. They eat them for lunch and use them to keep their hands warm on the way to work.	15 30 45 58 74
On their way to work, Jo tries to cheer up Meg. Jo talks about what she will do for her sisters when she is rich.	90 99
Even though they are young, they work. Their father lost his fortune helping a friend, so Meg works as a nanny and Jo is a companion for their great aunt. Their aunt is cranky, but as soon as she falls asleep, Jo can read the books in her uncle's library.	111 127 142 149
Jo is ambitious and wants to be famous. She knows she is going to do something great and wonderful. She first has to learn to control her temper.	164 177
In Chapter 4, the reader learns that Beth is too shy to go to school so her parents home school her. But since her father is away and her mother is helping poor people, she is supposed to do her lessons on her own. Beth spends a lot of time helping Hannah around the house and playing dolls. She has a collection of dolls, in various states of repair, that her sisters have discarded. Beth loves to play the piano, but her family only has a really old one that is out of tune and needs to be repaired.	193 207 221 234 249 264 275
The reader also discovers that Amy is vain. The sisters have natural pairings. Meg and Amy have a special bond. Jo and Beth have a special bond.	287 301 302
In the evening, the girls and their mother sit around and talk about their day and tell stories. The girls especially like to listen to their mother's stories and promise her they will try to remember the lessons she teaches them.	316 330 343

Total Words Read: _____
Minus errors: _____
= CWPM _____

Name: _____   Date: _____

Fluency – Chapter 5 (4.2)

This is a one-minute timed reading. When time is up calculate the total CWPM read by using the formula at the bottom of the page.

Chapter 5 is titled *Being Neighborly*. Jo notices that Laurie studies inside	12
a lot. She gets the idea to go over and tell his grandfather that Laurie needs	28
to have more fun. When the chapter begins Jo thinks of Mr. Laurence as	42
"Old Mr. Laurence". As the chapter progresses that change and Jo develops	56
a fondness for him.	59
When Mr. Laurence is not home Jo throws a snowball at Laurie's window.	71
She finds out he can't go outside because he is sick. Jo decides to go read to	88
him. She goes and asks her mother if it would be okay for her to go next	105
door and her mother says yes. Jo goes back to the Laurence house. She	119
brings with her good wishes from her mother. Meg sends a dessert and Beth	133
her kittens for Laurie to play with. These gifts cheer Laurie up. Jo makes	147
him feel even better by straightening up his room a bit.	158
Jo offers to read to Laurie. He would rather talk. Jo is surprised that	172
Laurie watches her family. He longs for what they have. Both of Laurie's	185
parents are dead. Laurie is cheered up by Jo's stories as she tells him about	200
her life. Jo invites Laurie to come over to her house when he is better.	214
They begin talking about books. Laurie tells Jo about his grandfather's	225
great library. The doctor comes to look in on Laurie and Jo goes to browse	240
in the library. In the library she is caught talking to herself. She is looking	255
at his portrait and says out loud that the old man looks stubborn, but kind.	270
Mr. Laurence finds this amusing. Mr. Laurence asks how Jo's mother is. Jo	283
tells him she is over taking care of the Hummels. Mr. Laurence invites Jo to	298
stay for tea. Mr. Laurence notices how happy his grandson is. Jo asks	311
Laurie to play the piano for her, but his grandfather cuts him off. His	325
grandfather is afraid that Laurie will be like his father – who ran off with a	340
musician and both of them were killed. Laurie playing the piano reminds	352
him of the person who caused the family to split apart.	363
Jo goes home and tells Marmee about her day. Marmee lets Jo know that	377
Laurie is welcome anytime.	381

Total Words Read: _____
Minus errors: _____
= CWPM _____

Name: _____   Date: _____

Fluency – Chapter 6

This is a one-minute timed reading. When time is up calculate the total CWPM read by using the formula at the bottom of the page.

Chapter 6 is titled: "Beth Finds the Palace Beautiful". Beth talks about the	13
lions keeping the March family from entering the "Palace Beautiful" – which	24
is Laurie's house. Beth is referring to Mr. Laurence. She finds him	36
intimidating. The other lion is that Mr. Laurence is wealthy and the March	49
family no longer has money.	54
Laurie has found best friends in the March family. He is constantly with	67
them. He is happier and peppier, but he is beginning to neglect his studies.	81
Mr. Laurence likes the change in Laurie and tells the boy's tutor to back off a	97
bit and let Laurie spend time with his friends.	106
As the chapter progresses, the girls overcome their fear of Mr. Laurence,	118
except for Beth. Mr. Laurence gets Beth over her fear with a wonderful	131
gesture. One day, Mr. Laurence goes to the March house and talks to Beth's	145
mother within earshot of Beth. With Beth listening, Mr. Laurence tells	156
Marmee that he would be grateful if one of the girls would come over and	172
play his great piano so it would get used. He says that the house is usually	188
deserted, so the person could slip in and out unnoticed.	198
Beth is so happy she can hardly stand it. The next morning she gets up,	213
does her housework and then goes over to the Laurence house. She spends	226
all day playing the piano.	231
Beth goes to the Laurence house nearly every day to play the piano. Beth	245
decides to make a thank you for Mr. Laurence for his kindness. She makes	259
him a pair of slippers. She leaves them for him in his study. In return for	275
the slippers, Mr. Laurence sends Beth a note along with his deceased	287
granddaughter's upright piano.	290
Beth knows that she must overcome her fear and thank Mr. Laurence for	303
the gift. She does it quickly, while she is still excited, so she won't lose her	319
nerve. She walks directly next door and into his study and thanks him.	332
They develop a bond like a grandfather and granddaughter.	341

Total Words Read: _____
Minus errors: _____
= CWPM   _____

Name: _____   Date: _____

Fluency – Chapter 7 (5.4)

This is a one-minute timed reading. When time is up calculate the total CWPM read by using the formula at the bottom of the page.

Chapter 7 is titled: *Amy's Valley of Humiliation.* Meg, Jo, Beth and Amy are	14
sitting at home. Laurie rides up on his horse. Amy admires how he rides.	28
She also admires his money. Meg and Jo ask Amy why she likes his money	43
so much and she says because it is fashionable at school for the girls to buy	59
and share pickled limes and if she had money could be fashionable too.	72
Amy has been given a lot of pickled limes from her classmates, but she	86
has not been able to return the favor because she doesn't have the money to	101
buy any. Meg gives Amy twenty-five cents. The next day Amy buys a paper	116
bag of 24 pickled limes. She shows them off before school begins and all of	131
the girls want to be her friend. A girl name Jenny Snow is rude to her	147
regularly, so Amy tells her she will not share with her. Jenny gets mad and	162
tells on Amy.	165
There is a rule at school – no pickled limes. The teacher is adamant about	179
it. He calls Amy to the front of the class and humiliates her. He makes her	195
throw her limes out of the window and he hits her with a yard stick. To add	112
to her humiliation he makes her stand in front of the class until recess.	226
She goes home and tells her family what happened. Marmee does not	238
agree with Amy's behavior, but she does not agree with the punishment	250
either. Marmee tells Amy she can continue her studies at home until her	263
father is back from the war and finds her another school.	274
Marmee tells Amy it was wrong to break the rules. Marmee also tells	287
Amy that she needs to try not to be so selfish and conceited.	300
Laurie and Jo are playing a board game in the corner of the room. When	315
Laurie leaves Amy asks her mother if she thinks Laurie is accomplished.	327
Marmee says yes, but adds that he is also polite and humble.	339

Total Words Read: _____
Minus errors: _____
= CWPM   _____

Name: _____   Date: _____

Fluency – Chapter 8 (3.6)

This is a one-minute timed reading. When time is up calculate the total CWPM read by using the formula at the bottom of the page.

Chapter 8 is titled: *Jo Meets Apollyon*. Meg and Jo are dressed in their nice	15
clothes. Amy sees them and wants to know where they are going. Jo does not	30
want to tell Amy. Amy begs and Meg tells her. Laurie is taking them to the	46
theater. They are going to see *The Seven Castles*. Amy wants to come. Her	60
sisters tell her that she is not invited and that she doesn't have a ticket.	75
Meg tries to make Amy feel better telling her that she will see the play	90
with Hannah and Beth, but Amy wants to go tonight. She wants to go with	105
Meg, Jo and Laurie.	109
Meg wants to give in to her, but Jo will not let her. Jo states that it will be	128
rude to Laurie. Amy says that she has her own money and could buy a	143
ticket. Jo points out that Laurie will be polite and give her his seat and then	159
he will have to sit alone and that isn't fair. Besides they want Laurie's	173
company, not Amy's. Amy tells Jo if she doesn't get to go Jo will be sorry.	189
The play is wonderful. When Meg and Jo get home Amy is silently	202
reading and doesn't speak to them. Beth asks about the play.	213
Jo looks for her manuscripts of original writings. It is missing. She asks	226
her sisters if they have seen it and they say no, but Amy looks guilty. Amy	241
admits that she destroyed it. It is Jo's only copy and she is furious. Marmee	256
comes home and helps Amy to see what a terrible and irreversible thing she	270
has done. Amy tries to apologize, but Jo will not forgive her. Not even	284
Marmee's encouragement can get Jo to accept Amy's apology.	293
The next day is a horrible one for Jo, so Laurie takes her ice skating. Amy	310
is mad because Jo promised to take her ice skating. She goes without	322
permission. As she is trying to catch up with Jo and Laurie she falls into the	338
pond. Laurie rescues her. She is fine and Jo forgives her.	349

Total Words Read: _____
Minus errors: _____
= CWPM _____

Name: _____   Date: _____

Fluency – Chapter 10 (4.5)

This is a one-minute timed reading. When time is up calculate the total CWPM read by using the formula at the bottom of the page.

Chapter 10 is titled: *The P.C. and the P.O.* This chapter contains many	13
references to <u>The Pickwick Papers</u> by Charles Dickens. Winter is over and	25
each girl gets to work part of the garden. Their garden's are each different.	39
Meg's is pretty. Jo likes doing experiment with hers. Beth grows things for	52
her pets and dolls. Amy's if fashionable and elegant.	61
On rainy days, the girls hold meetings of the P.C. or Pickwick Club. At	75
the time <u>Little Women</u> was written, people were forming Pickwick Clubs. The	87
Pickwick Club from the book has the characters reporting on their travels	99
through Europe. Each of the girls takes a character from the book to be	114
during their "club time". Their club is exclusively for girls. They publish a	127
paper in their club. The paper includes poems and jokes. It includes a	140
romantic tale, recipes and various other announcements.	147
After they read the newspaper aloud Jo gets up and says she would like	161
to admit a new member. She wants to add Laurie. Beth and Jo want to	176
admit Laurie. Meg and Amy are against it. Meg is worried Laurie will make	190
fun of them. Amy doesn't want to play with a boy. Beth and Jo convince	204
them to let Laurie be a member. It is a good thing, because, Laurie was	219
hiding in a closet listening the whole time. The sisters are mad at Jo, until	235
Laurie proves he understands the book and announces he will play Sam	247
Weller.	248
Laurie also lets the girls know that he is going to give them a post office	264
box in the middle of the hedge between their homes. They will be able to	279
exchanges letters for the club and for fun. Laurie has a key and gives the	294
girls a key.	297

Total Words Read: _____
Minus errors: _____
= CWPM   _____

Name: _____   Date: _____

Fluency – Chapter 11 (4.4)

This is a one-minute timed reading. When time is up calculate the total CWPM read by using the formula at the bottom of the page.

Chapter 11 is titled: *Experiments.* This chapter opens with Meg and Jo	12
happy to have the summer free of work. Meg plans to laze around. Jo has a	27
pile of books she wants to read. They are excited for the summer. The girls	42
get the idea that they want to take a break from all of their housework and	58
other chores.	60
The next day Meg gets up late, sits around and then goes shopping. Beth	74
plays with her dolls and makes a big mess and doesn't clean it up. Jo reads	90
all day and gives herself a headache. Amy decides to go for a walk to do	107
some drawing, but it rains and she ends up getting all wet.	119
That evening the girls talk about how great the day was. They also talk	133
about how long it seemed. They tell their mom that their experiment is	145
working well. Marmee just smiles to herself and doesn't say anything about	157
their experiment. Marmee and Hannah do all of the chores and housework.	169
By Friday, the girls will not admit it but they are happy the experiment is	184
almost over. They wake up on Saturday to discover that Marmee is going to	198
stay in her room all day and that she has given Hannah the day off. No one	215
does the chores or the housework.	221
The girls try to make breakfast for their mother but they are not good	234
cooks. Jo decides to invite Laurie over for lunch. Beth discovers that she	247
has neglected her pet bird and that he is dead.	257
Meg's friends come over and so does a friend of the family who	270
announces that she is there for lunch as well. The lunch is a mess. The food	286
tastes horrible. Laurie tries to make everyone feel better. They finally get to	299
the end of the meal to discover that Jo put salt on the fruit instead of sugar.	216
Jo is about to cry, but Laurie makes light of it and they all laugh.	231
At the end of the day Marmee comes out and teaches them a lesson	245
about all working together and each person doing their part. Each of the	258
girls decides to learn something new.	264

Total Words Read: _____
Minus errors: _____
= CWPM   _____

Name: _____   Date: _____

Fluency – Chapter 12 (5.1)

This is a one-minute timed reading. When time is up calculate the total CWPM read by using the formula at the bottom of the page.

Chapter 12 is titled: *Camp Laurence*. Beth is delivering the "mail" from	12
their "Post Office" and there is an invitation from Laurie for all of them to	27
join him for a picnic the next day. He will be entertaining friends from	42
England. There will be four children. Kate is a little older than Meg, twins,	56
Fred and Frank are Jo's age and Grace is around Amy's age. Beth doesn't	70
want to go because she is shy, but Laurie says she must.	81
They wake up the next morning and go to the picnic. They set off for the	97
picnic site in several boats. Beth feels compassion for, and develops a bond	110
with, Frank because he is sickly. Amy and Grace hit it off well, but Kate is a	127
little bit conceited. Some of their other friends come along as well and so	141
does Mr. Brooke, Laurie's tutor.	146
While playing croquet Jo gets angry because Fred cheats. Jo keeps her	158
temper, because she has promised Marmee she will try, and Laurie and Meg	171
congratulate her for doing so. Jo wins for her team, despite the cheating.	184
They also play a story-telling game called "Rig-marole". One person	195
begins a story and breaks off at an exciting point, the next person must	209
finish the story. Mr. Brooke begins the story at Meg's request. They play	222
several more games but Meg and Kate sit out. While they are doing so, Kate	237
becomes a braggart about speaking German, but Mr. Brooke turns it around	248
and praises Meg.	251
Mr. Brooke tells Meg that he is going to enlist in the Civil War. Meg is	267
glad he is going to serve his country.	275
After the March sisters return home, Kate says that American girls are	287
nice once you get to know them and Mr. Brooke agrees with her.	300

Total Words Read: _____
Minus errors: _____
= CWPM   _____

Name: _____   Date: _____

Fluency – Chapter 13 (5.4)

This is a one-minute timed reading. When time is up calculate the total CWPM read by using the formula at the bottom of the page.

Chapter 13 is titled: *Castles in the Air.* One day Laurie spots the girls	14
dressed as they walk by his house. He thinks they are going on a picnic	29
without him, so he follows them. He discovers the sisters in a little grove	43
where each girl is working on a project. Amy is drawing, Beth sorting cones	57
for crafts, Meg sewing and Jo knitting and reading – all at the same time.	71
At first they don't want Laure there. But then they relent and let him stay	86
as long as he does something, so he decides to read to them.	99
The girls explain that they are still playing "Pilgrim's Progress. They tell	111
him that he hill they are on is "The Delectable Mountain". It is so because	126
they can see all around them and dream about where they are going to live	141
someday. They start talking about castles and dreams and what each of	153
their "Castle in the Air" is specifically.	160
Laurie wants to have fun and be a famous musician and live in Germany.	174
Meg wants luxurious things and to be fashionable. Jo wants a herd of	187
Arabian horses and stacks of books. Beth wants to stay home with her	200
family and take care of them. Amy wants to live in Rome and be an artist.	216
Laurie says he has the key to his castle but can't use it because he has to	232
go to college. Jo thoughtlessly advises him to "sail away" in one of his own	247
ships until he has accomplished his dreams. Meg disagrees and tells Jo to	261
stop. She reminds them all that Laurie's grandfather is kind and well	273
meaning.	274
When Laurie gets home he sees him watching Beth plays the piano and	287
decides he needs to stay home because his grandfather needs him.	298

Total Words Read: _____
Minus errors: _____
= CWPM _____

Name: _____   Date: _____

Fluency – Chapter 14 (3.6)

This is a one-minute timed reading. When time is up calculate the total CWPM read by using the formula at the bottom of the page.

Chapter 14 is titled: *Secrets*. In this chapter, Jo secretly takes a	12
story to a newspaper publisher. Laurie catches her being sneaky and he	24
tells her if she tells him what she was doing, he will tell her a secret. They	41
exchange secrets and his deeply disturbs Jo. Laurie's secret is that Brooke	53
is the person who kept Meg's missing love and that Mr. Brooke is in love	68
with Meg. He thinks Jo will be pleased. Jo is not pleased at all but very	84
upset.	85
To make her feel better Laurie suggests that they run down the hill. They	99
do. Jo's hair goes flying. It scatters her hairpins everywhere. Meg bumps	112
into them and is upset about Jo's "childish behavior" Jo proclaims that she	125
wants to stay a child as long as she can. She would like Meg to as well and	143
is about to say as much when Laurie interrupts.	152
Laurie asks Meg where she has been. Meg says she was visiting Sallie	165
Gardner. They were talking about Belle Moffat's wedding.	173
She begins to act strangely, treating Mr. Brooke coldly and staring sadly	185
at Meg. One day, Jo comes in with Laurie. They are excited. Jo reads them	200
all a story from the newspaper. They ask who wrote it. Jo says she did. They	216
are very excited for her. Jo explains that she wasn't paid for this story, but	231
she will be for others.	236

Total Words Read: _____
Minus errors: _____
= CWPM _____

Name: _____   Date: _____

Fluency – Chapter 15 (3.6)

This is a one-minute timed reading. When time is up calculate the total CWPM read by using the formula at the bottom of the page.

Chapter 15 is titled: *Telegram*. The girls are sitting at home on a cold	14
day. Meg is feeling poor and sorry for herself that she has to work so hard. It	31
is November again. Jo and Amy try to comfort her. They tell her when they	46
are rich they will share. Jo will be a famous writer and Amy will be a famous	63
artist.	64
A telegram arrives. It is about their father. Mr. March has been taken	77
sick. The telegram says that Marmee she should come to Washington	88
immediately. Everyone rushes around trying to help her. Marmee asks	98
Laurie to take a letter to Aunt March as Marmee borrows money for the trip.	113
Mr. Laurence sends Mr. Brooke on the trip so Marmee has an escort.	126
Marmee is pleased. Mr. Laurence also gives her wine to nurse Mr. March	139
back to health	142
Aunt March sends back the money Marmee asks for. She also sends a	155
note that says "I told you so." Everyone is has finished getting Marmee ready	170
and are about to have tea when Jo comes in – without her hair. She sold it	185
for $25 to help out. Jo saved one lock of hair for her mother to keep. Jo has	203
trouble admitting it but she feels that she has sold her one beautiful trait.	217
They all go to bed, except Marmee. Marmee roams the house, kisses	229
her girls and prays.	233

Total Words Read: _____
Minus errors: _____
= CWPM _____

Name: _____   Date: _____

Fluency – Chapter 16 (3.5)

This is a one-minute timed reading. When time is up calculate the total CWPM read by using the formula at the bottom of the page.

Chapter 16 is titled: *Letters*. The girls are up early. They go down to	14
breakfast and try to be strong for Marmee. Marmee is positive and	26
encourages the girls as she prepares to leave. Hannah will take care of them	40
and Mr. Laurence says that he will make sure the girls are cared for and	55
safe. The girls cry for a bit after their mother leaves. They have breakfast	69
and feel better. Beth and Amy help with the housework. Meg and Jo go off to	85
work.	86
Much of the chapter is written in the form of letters back and forth	100
between Marmee and her family and the Laurences. The first letter is from	113
Meg. Meg tells Marmee that everyone is being good and that each of her	127
sisters is behaving. She also tells her mother that Mr. Laurence is looking	140
after them.	142
Jo's letter is next. Jo's letter is not nearly as formal as Meg's. Actually,	156
each letter takes on the character traits of its author. Jo adds a funny	170
poem. It is about housework. She is trying to cheer up her father.	182
Beth's letter is short and sweet. She sends her father some fresh flowers.	195
She also tells her mother that she is behaving and doing what she is	209
supposed to. Amy adds to Beth's letter. Her section is poorly written. She	222
complains about Laurie teasing her. Laurie writes and signs his name as	234
"Colonel Teddy". It is obvious they all miss Marmee.	243
The last letter is a short note from Mr. Laurence. He tells Mrs. March that	258
everything is going well. He again offers any help that Mr. March needs.	271

Total Words Read: _____
Minus errors: _____
= CWPM   _____

Name: _____   Date: _____

Fluency – Chapter 17 (3.5)

This is a one-minute timed reading. When time is up calculate the total CWPM read by using the formula at the bottom of the page.

Chapter 17 is titled: *Little Faithful.* After only a week of Marmee	12
being gone, the Meg, Jo and Amy being to neglect their duties. It seems their	27
promises to Marmee to keeps things running as usual are forgotten. Beth	39
hasn't forgotten. She is still doing her work. She is also doing some of her	54
sister's work as well. One of the things she is doing faithfully is visiting the	69
poor family Marmee helps to care for. Only now the baby is sick. Beth	83
becomes very tired. She asks one of her sisters to go visit with the family. It	99
is draining her. Each of her sisters has an excuse of why they can't go, so	115
Beth goes again.	118
Jo comes home that day. She finds Beth upstairs alone. Beth explains	130
to her that the baby died in her arms of scarlet fever. She is afraid that she	147
may get it and she doesn't feel well. Since a person can only get scarlet fever	163
once, and Meg and Jo have already had it, they are safe. Amy has never had	178
it, so she is in danger. They send Amy off to live with Aunt March to protect	194
her. When Laurie comes to visit, he finds Amy crying on the couch. He asks	209
her what is wrong. She tells him what happened. Laurie promises to visit	222
her every day.	225
Laurie asks if he should telegram Marmee, but they don't want to	237
worry her so they say no. They call for Dr. Bangs. He confirms that Beth is	253
sick. Amy is depressed that she has to stay several weeks with Aunt March.	267

Total Words Read: _____
Minus errors: _____
= CWPM   _____

Name: _____   Date: _____

Fluency – Chapter 19

This is a one-minute timed reading. When time is up calculate the total CWPM read by using the formula at the bottom of the page.

Chapter 19 is titled: *Amy's Will*. Aunt March tries to be nice to Amy. Aunt March is cranky, but she likes her great-niece. In fact, she seems to like her a lot. Still, Amy has a rough time not being home. Aunt March tries to occupy Amy's time by giving her chores to do. Amy loves when Laurie visits. Amy also likes to explore the house. Esther, the maid, is kind and allows her to look though her aunt's closet and jewelry.	15 28 39 54 68 81 94
During one of these sessions, Esther asks Amy which piece she would choose for herself if she could. Although she first selects a string of gold and ebony beads, Esther tells her that Aunt March has already declared that Amy will get the turquoise ring. This prospect gives Amy the courage to endure her aunt's discipline. She becomes a near perfect child. With the help of the maid, Amy creates a prayer room for herself where she goes when she needs to feel better.	102 116 128 141 155 171 184 196
Amy begins to think about the idea of a will. Amy decides to create a will of her one. In her will she gives Jo her most prized possessions because she burned Jo's book of original stories. It is obvious that this fact still haunts her. Laurie comes to visit and Amy tells him about her will. She has Laurie sign as a witness. Amy asks Laurie if Beth is going to die. Laurie comforts Amy.	

Total Words Read: _____
Minus errors: _____
= CWPM   _____

Name: _____   Date: _____

Fluency – Chapter 20

This is a one-minute timed reading. When time is up calculate the total CWPM read by using the formula at the bottom of the page.

Chapter 20 is titled: *Confidential*. The girls, along with Laurie and Mr.	12
Laurence, are excited Marmee is home. Marmee visits Amy at the Aunt	24
March's house. Marmee mother encourages her daughter and tells her she	35
will be able to come home soon. Amy shows her mother the ring Aunt March	50
has already given her. She is very proud of it. Amy begs to be allowed to wear	67
it as a reminder to keep from being selfish.	76
Mrs. March confides in Jo. She tells her daughter that Mr. Brooke, who	89
she now calls "John", has asked permission to court Meg. When Meg is	102
older of course. This does not make Jo happy. Jo wants Meg to marry	116
Laurie. Jo has a difficult time thinking about any of her sisters moving	129
outside of their family unit. She doesn't ever want anything to change.	141
Marmee makes Jo promise that she won't tell Meg anything about their	153
conversation or about John's feelings. Jo thinks about some of the things	165
Meg has said and done in the past. Jo realizes that her sister may be falling	181
in love with John.	185
Meg comes into the room and Jo goes to bed. Meg shows Marmee a letter	200
to her father. Marmee asks her to add a statement sending her love to John.	215
Meg is pleased. Meg goes to bed. Marmee thinks to herself that her daughter	229
will soon be in love with John Brooke.	236

Total Words Read: _____
Minus errors: _____
= CWPM _____

Name: _____   Date: _____

Fluency – Chapter 21(4.2)

This is a one-minute timed reading. When time is up calculate the total CWPM read by using the formula at the bottom of the page.

Chapter 21 is titled: *Laurie Makes Mischief Jo Makes Peace.* Jo keeps her	13
promise to Marmee. She does not talk to Meg about John Brooke. Meg can	27
tell that Jo is keeping something from her, but she doesn't know what it is.	42
Laurie can also tell that Jo is keeping a secret. Laurie pushes and pushes	56
until he guesses that it is about John and Meg. Jo will not tell Laurie the	72
details. Laurie decides he is going to get back at Jo for keeping the secret.	87
He writes a series of letters to Meg and pretends they are from John Brooke.	102
Meg responds that she is too young to marry.	112
One day, Jo delivers another letter to Meg from their pretend "Post	124
Office." It is sealed. It makes Meg blush. Marmee gets it out of Meg that	139
John received her reply, to the letter that he didn't write. Meg thinks Jo did	154
it. When Jo examines the fraudulent letters, she knows it is Laurie. Marmee	167
sends Jo to get Laurie. When Jo is gone, Marmee tells Meg about John's	181
feelings and his request to court her when she is older. Jo and Meg are	196
called back into the room and Laurie apologizes.	204
Mr. Laurence knows something is wrong. He gets angry at Laurie. Laurie	216
promised Marmee he wouldn't talk about what happened, so he does not.	228
Laurie overreacts when his grandfather gets angry and says he is going to	241
run away. Jo goes to Mr. Laurence and explains about Marmee. Jo gets Mr.	255
Laurence to apologize to Laurie. Back at the March house, Meg is starting to	269
have romantic feelings for John Brooke.	275

Total Words Read: _____
Minus errors: _____
= CWPM _____

Name: _____   Date: _____

Fluency – Chapter 22 (5.5)

This is a one-minute timed reading. When time is up calculate the total CWPM read by using the formula at the bottom of the page.

Chapter 22 is titled: *Pleasant Meadows*. The girls, Marmee and Hannah	11
celebrate another Christmas. This time Laurie is with them. Beth is better.	23
She has moved from her bed to the living room sofa. Amy is home from Aunt	39
March's house. Unlike last year, each girl receives a gift of something she	52
really wants.	54
Marmee receives a letter from her husband saying he will soon home.	66
They don't realize how soon. They are surprised and delighted when John	78
Brooke and their father arrive home. He still has some weak, but is able to	93
sit in an easy chair along with Beth and enjoy the company of the family.	108
Laurie, Mr. Laurence and Mr. Brooke enjoy Christmas dinner with them. In	120
spite of the happiness of the occasion, Jo cannot resist glaring at Mr.	133
Brooke.	134
As they sit down to eat, Mr. March comments on the changes in his	148
daughters. He observes that Amy is less selfish, Jo acts more like a lady and	163
is more polite and that Meg has hands that are not useless and soft. Her	179
hands show signs of productive housework. He also notes that Beth is not	192
as shy as she once was, although Mr. March is afraid to say much about	207
Beth for fear she will "slip away altogether". This observation is a bit of	221
foreshadowing and ends the otherwise happy chapter on an ominous note.	232
The chapter actually ends with Beth playing the piano and singing. It has	245
been a long time since she was able to do that and life is good in the March	263
home.	264

Total Words Read: _____
Minus errors: _____
= CWPM   _____

Name: _____   Date: _____

Fluency – Chapter 23 (2.6)

This is a one-minute timed reading. When time is up calculate the total CWPM read by using the formula at the bottom of the page.

Chapter 23 is titled: *Aunt March Settles the Question.* It is the day after	14
Christmas. The girls, Marmee and Hannah are glad Mr. March is home. They	27
spend much of their time taking care of him.	36
One day, Laurie comes in, gets down on his knee and imitates the way	50
John Brooks is going to propose to Meg. Meg tells him that she doesn't care	65
about John. Jo is disgusted with her sister and believes she is lying. Meg	79
gets frustrated with Jo for talking about it so much. Jo asks Meg what she	94
would do if John proposed. Meg tells her she would refuse. Jo is very	107
pleased by this and makes John promise that she will turn John down.	121
John comes by to pick up an umbrella he has forgotten. Meg and Jo look	136
startled and a bit guilty when he comes in. Jo leaves so that Meg can turn	152
him down in private. Meg thanks John for taking care of her father. He	166
takes her hand. Meg becomes nervous. John finally asks what he has come	179
to ask. John asks if she cares for him.	188
Meg now sees that John is nervous. This makes her confident. She begins	201
to act coyly. She tells him he should go. John is hurt. He asks if that is what	219
she truly wants. He asks Meg to be honest and tells her he is willing to wait	236
for her.	238
Aunt March comes in. She sees Meg and John together and demands an	251
explanation. John leaves the room. Meg tells her aunt that John Brooke is a	266
friend of her fathers. Aunt March recognizes the name. She knows who John	279
Brooke is. She also knows he is interested in Meg. Aunt March tells Meg it is	295
her duty to marry rich. She also says that as the oldest niece she could	309
inherit her aunt's fortune, but won't if she marries John. Meg is offended.	322
These comments push Meg towards John. Meg realizes that she must care	334
about John more than she thought.	340
Jo comes out when John and Meg are alone together again and she	353
catches a private conversation. All find out that Meg and John will be	366
married in three years. Laurie wonders where they will all really be in three	370
years' time.	372

Total Words Read: _____
Minus errors: _____
= CWPM   _____